The Leverage Space Trading Model

Founded in 1807, John Wiley & Sons is the oldest independent publishing company in the United States. With offices in North America, Europe, Australia, and Asia, Wiley is globally committed to developing and marketing print and electronic products and services for our customers' professional and personal knowledge and understanding.

The Wiley Trading series features books by traders who have survived the market's ever changing temperament and have prospered—some by reinventing systems, others by getting back to basics. Whether a novice trader, professional or somewhere in-between, these books will provide the advice and strategies needed to prosper today and well into the future.

For a list of available titles, visit our Web site at www.WileyFinance.com.

The Leverage Space Trading Model

Reconciling Portfolio Management Strategies and Economic Theory

RALPH VINCE

WILEY

John Wiley & Sons, Inc.

Published by John Wiley & Sons, Inc., Hoboken, New Jersey.
Published simultaneously in Canada.

For general information on our other products and services or for technical support, please contact our Customer Care Department within the United States at (800) 762-2974, outside the United States at (317) 572-3993 or fax (317) 572-4002.

Wiley also publishes its books in a variety of electronic formats. Some content that appears in print may not be available in electronic books. For more information about Wiley products, visit our web site at www.wiley.com.

Library of Congress Cataloging-in-Publication Data:

Vince, Ralph, 1958–
The leverage space trading model : reconciling portfolio management strategies and economic theory / Ralph Vince.
    p. cm. – (Wiley trading series)
  Includes bibliographical references and index.
  ISBN 978-0-470-45595-1 (cloth)
  1. Portfolio management.   2. Investment analysis.   3. Investments.   I. Title.
  HG4529.5.V558 2209
  332.601–dc22   2009000839

Printed in the United States of America.

10 9 8 7 6 5 4 3 2 1

He that will not apply new remedies must expect new evils; for time is the greatest innovator.

—Francis Bacon

Contents

Preface

I can explain...
This material began as a panoply of notes for a series of talks I gave in late 2007 and in 2008, after the publication of *The Handbook of Portfolio Mathematics.*

In those talks, I spoke of how there exists a plethora of market analysis, selection and timing techniques including charts and fundamental analysis, trading systems, Elliot waves, and on and on—all sorts of models and methods, technical and otherwise, to assist in timing and selection.

You wouldn't initiate a trade without using the analysis you specialize in, but there is another world, a world of quantity, a world "out there someplace," which has either been dark and unknown or, at best, fraught with heuristics. You will begin to understand this as I show you how those heuristics have evolved and are, very often, just plain wrong. Numerous Nobel Prizes have been awarded based on some of those widely accepted principles. I am referring specifically to the contemporary techniques of combining assets into a portfolio and determining their relative quantities. These widely accepted approaches, however, are wrong and will get you into trouble. I will show you how and why that is. They illuminate nothing, aside from providing the illusion of safety through diversification. In the netherworld of quantity, those flawed techniques still leave us in the dark.

There are still fund managers out there who use those atavistic techniques. They stumble blindly along the dim, twisted pathways of that netherworld. This is akin to trading without your charts, systems, or other analytical tools. Yet most of the world does just that. (See Figure P.1.)

And whether you acknowledge it or not, it *is* at work on you, just as gravity is at work on you.

Pursuing my passion for this material, I found there is an entire *domain* that I have sought to catalogue, regarding quantity, which is just as important as the discipline of timing and selection. This other area is shrouded in darkness and mystery, absent a framework or even a coordinate system. Once I could apply a viable framework, I found this dark netherworld alive with fascinating phenomena and bubbling with geometrical relationships.

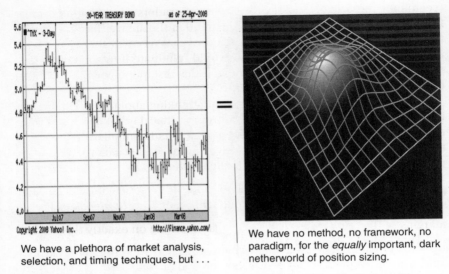

We have a plethora of market analysis, selection, and timing techniques, but . . .

We have no method, no framework, no paradigm, for the *equally* important, dark netherworld of position sizing.

FIGURE P.1   Market Analysis and Position Sizing (Both Equally Necessary)

Most importantly, the effects of our actions regarding quantity decisions were illuminated.

I have encountered numerous frustrations while trying to make this point since the publication of *Portfolio Management Formulas* in 1990: People are lazy. They want a card they can put into a bank machine and get money. Very few want to put forth the mental effort to think, or to endure the necessary psychological pain to think outside of their comfortable, self-imposed boxes. They remain trapped within their suffocating, limited mental notions of how things should operate. Incidentally, I do not claim immunity from this.

When I alluded to quantity as the "other, necessary half" of trading, I was being overly generous, even apologetic about it. After all, some of the members of my audiences were revered market technicians and notable panjandrums. Indeed, I believe that quantity is nearly 100 percent of the matter, not merely half, and I submit that you are perhaps better off to disregard your old means of analysis, timing, and selection altogether.

Yes, I said *100 percent*.

On Saturday, 26 January 2008, I was having lunch in the shadow of Tokyo Tower with Hiroyuki Narita, Takaaki Sera, and Masaki Nagasawa. Hiro stirred the conversation with something I had only marginally had bubbling in my head for the past few years.

He said something, almost in passing, about what he really needed as a trader. It knocked me over. I knew, suddenly, instantly, that what he was

(seemingly rhetorically) asking for is what all traders need, that it is something that no one has really addressed, and that the answer has likely been
floating in the ether all around us. I knew at that moment that if I thought
about this, got my arms around it, it would fulminate into something that
would change how I viewed everything in this discipline which I had been
obsessed with for decades.

In the following days, I could not stop thinking about this. Those guys
in Tokyo didn't have to do a hard sell on me that day. I knew they were
right, and that everything I had worked on and had compulsively stored in
a corner of my mind for decades was (even more so) just a mere framework
upon which to construct what was really needed.

I might have been content to stay holed up in my little fort along the
Chagrin River, but an entirely new thread was beginning to reveal itself.

On the flight home, in the darkness of the plane, unable to sleep, in the
margins of the book I was reading, I began working on exactly this.

That's where this book is going.

RALPH VINCE
Selby Library, Sarasota
August 2008

Introduction

T his is a storybook, not a textbook. It is the story of ideas that go back roughly three centuries, and how they have, and continue, to change. It is the story of how resources should be combined, when confronted with one or more prospects of uncertain outcome, where the amount of such resources you will have for the next prospect of uncertain outcome is dependent on what occurs with this outcome. In other words, your resources are not replenished from outside.

It is a story that ultimately must answer the question, "What are you looking to accomplish at the end of this process, and *how* do you plan to implement it?" The answer to this question is vitally important because it dictates what kinds of actions we should take. Given the complex and seemingly pathological character of human desires, we are presented with a fascinating puzzle within a story that has some interesting twists and turns, one of which is about to take place.

There are some who might protest, "Some of this was published earlier!" They would certainly be correct. A lot of the material herein presents concepts that I have previously discussed. However, they are necessary parts of the thread of this story and are provided not only for that reason but also in consideration of those readers who are not familiar with these concepts. Those who *are* familiar with the past concepts, peppered throughout Parts I and II of this story, can gloss over them as we build with them in Part III.

As mentioned in the Preface, this material began as a panoply of notes for a series of talks I gave in late 2007 and in 2008 after the publication of *The Handbook of Portfolio Mathematics* (which, in turn, built upon previous things I had written of, along with notes of things pertaining to drawdowns, which I had begun working on in my spare time while at the Abu Dhabi Investment Authority, a first-rate institution consisting of first-rate and generous individuals whom I had the extreme good fortune to be employed by some years ago). I designed those talks to illustrate the concepts in the book, in a manner that made them simpler, more intuitive, essentially devoid of mathematics and, therefore, more easily digestible. I have drawn from those talks and fleshed them out further for this book, with their mathematical derivations and explanations of *how* to perform them. This comprises a good portion of the early sections of this text. This background, at least conceptually, is necessary to understand the new material.

One idea, discussed at length in the past, needs to be discussed before we begin the story. It is the concept of *Mathematical Expectation*. This is called "Expected Value," by some, and it represents what we would expect to make, on average, per play, when faced with a given "prospect"—an outcome we cannot yet know, which may be favorable or not. The concept is introduced in 1657 in a treatise by the Dutch Mathematician and Physicist Christian Huygens, at the prompting of Blaise Pascal.

This value, the Mathematical Expectation (ME), is simply the sum of the products of the probabilities and payoffs of all the ways something might turn out:

$$ME = \sum_{i=1}^{n} (P_i * A_i)$$

where: P_i = the probability associated with the ith outcome
           A_i = the result of the ith outcome
           n = the total number of possible outcomes

For example, assume we toss a coin and if it's heads we win two units and if it's tails we lose one unit. There are two possible outcomes, $+2$ and -1, each with a probability of 0.5.

An *ME* of 0 is said to be a "fair" gamble. If *ME* is positive, it is said to be a favorable gamble, and if negative, a losing gamble. Note that *in a game with a negative ME (that is, most gambling games), the probability of going broke approaches certainty as you continue to play.*

The equation for Mathematical Expectation, or "expected value," is quite foundational to studying this discipline.

Mathematical Expectation is a cornerstone to our story here. Not only is it a cornerstone to gambling theory, it is also a cornerstone to principles in Game Theory, wherein payoff matrices are often assessed based on Mathematical Expectation, as well as the discipline known as Economic Theory. Repeatedly in Economic Theory we see the notion of Mathematical Expectation transformed by the theory posited. We shall see this in Chapter 6.

However prevalent and persistent the notion of Mathematical Expectation, it must be looked at and used with the lens of a given horizon, a given lifespan. Frequently, viable methods are disregarded by otherwise-intelligent men because they show a negative Mathematical Expectation (and vice versa). This indicates a misunderstanding of the basic concept of Mathematical Expectation.

By way of example, let us assume a given lottery that is played once a week. We will further assume you are going to bet $1 on this lottery. Let us further assume you are a young man, and you plan to play this for 50 years. Thus, you expect $52 * 50 = 2,600$ plays you will be able to make.

Now let's say that this particular lottery has a one-in-two-million chance of winning a $1 million jackpot (this is for mere illustrative purposes, most lotteries having much lower probabilities of winning. For example, "Powerball," as presently played in the United States, has less than a 1-in-195,000,000 chance of winning its jackpot). Thus we see a negative expectation in our example lottery of:

$$1/2,000,000 * 1,000,000 + 1,999,999/2,000,000 * -1 = -0.4999995$$

Thus, we expect to lose $-$0.4999995$ per week, on average, playing this lottery (and based on this, we would expect to lose over the course of the 50 years we were to play this, $2,600 * -0.4999995 = -$1,300$).

Mathematical Expectation, however, is simply the "average," outcome (i.e., it is the mean of this distribution of the ways the future plays might turn out). In the instant case, we are discussing the outcome of 2,600 plays taken from a pool of two million possible plays, allowing for sample and replacement. Thus, the probability of seeing the single winning play in any randomly chosen 2,600 is:

$$1/2,000,000 * 2,600 = .0000005 * 2,600 = .0013$$

From this, we can say that $(1 - .0013 = .9987)$ 99.87 percent of the people who play this lottery every week for the next 50 years will lose $2,600. About 1/8 of 1 percent (.0013) will win $1 million (thus netting $1,000,000 - 2,600 = $997,400$). Clearly the mode of the distribution of outcomes for these 2,600 plays is to lose $2,600, even though the mean, as given by the Mathematical Expectation, is to lose $1,300.

Now, let's reverse things. Suppose now we have one chance in a million of winning $2 million. Now our Mathematical Expectation is:

$$1/1,000,000 * 2,000,000 + 999,999/1,000,000 * -1 = 1.000001$$

A positive expectation. If our sole criteria was to find a positive expectation, you would think we should accept this gamble. However, now the probability of seeing the single winning play in any randomly chosen 2,600 is:

$$1/1,000,000 * 2,600 = .000001 * 2,600 = .0026$$

In this positive expectation game, we can expect 99.74 percent of the people who play this over the next 50 years to lose $2,600. So is this positive expectation game a "good bet?" Is it a bet you would play expecting to make $1.000001 every week?

To drive home this important point we shall reverse the parameters of this game one more time. Assume a lottery wherein you are given $1 every week, with a one-in-one-million chance of losing $2 million. The Mathematical Expectation then is:

$$999,999/1,000,000 * 1 + 1/1,000,000 * -2,000,000 = -1.000001$$

Thus, we expect to lose −1.000001 per week, on average, playing this lottery (and based on this, we would expect to lose over the course of the 50 years we were to play this, $2,600 * -1.000001 = -\$2,600$).

Do we thus play this game, accept this proposition, given its negative Mathematical Expectation? Consider the probability that the 2,600 weeks we play this for will see the two million loss:

$$1/1,000,000 * 2,600 = 0.000001 * 2,600 = .0026$$

Thus, we would expect that 99.74 percent (1 − .0026) of the people who play this game will never see the $2 million loss. Instead, they will be given a dollar every week for 2,600 weeks. Thus, about 399 out of every 400 people who play this game will not see the one-in-a-million chance of losing $2 million over the course of 2,600 plays.

I trace out a path through 3D space not only of the places I go, but on a planet that revolves roughly once every 24 hours, about a heliocentric orbit of a period of roughly 365 1/4 days, in a solar system that is migrating through a galaxy, in a galaxy that is migrating through a universe, which itself is expanding.

Within this universe is an arbitrary-sized chunk of matter, making its own tangled path through 3D space. There is a point in time where my head and this object will attempt to occupy the same location in 3D space. The longer I live, the more certain I will see that moment.

Will I live long enough to see that moment? Likely not. That bet is a sure thing; however, its expectation approaches 1.0 as the length of my life approaches infinity. Do you want to accept that bet?

Clearly, Mathematical Expectation, a cornerstone of gambling theory, of money management as well as Economic Theory, must be utilized with the lens of a given horizon, a given lifespan. Hence the often-overlooked caveat in the definition provided earlier for Mathematical Expectation, "as you continue to play."

Often you will see the variable N throughout. This refers to the number of components in a portfolio, or the number of games played simultaneously. This is not to be confused with the lowercase n, which typically herein will refer to the total number of ways something might turn out.

Readers of the previous books will recognize the term "market system," which I have used with ubiquity. This is simply a given approach applied to a given market. Thus, I can be trading the same market with two different approaches, and therefore have two separate market systems. On the other hand, I can be trading a basket of markets with the same system and then have a basket of market systems. Typically, a market system is one component in a portfolio (and the distribution of outcomes of a market system is the same as the distribution of prices of the market comprising it, only transformed by the rules of the system comprising it).

Some of the ideas discussed herein are not employed, nor is there a reason to employ them. Among these ideas is the construction of the mean-variance portfolio model. Readers are referred to other works on these topics, and in the instant case, to Vince (1992).

I want to keep a solitary thread of reasoning running throughout the text, rather than a thread with multiple tentacles, which, ultimately, is redundant to things I have written of previously. Any redundancy in this text is intentional and used for the purpose of creating a clean, solitary thread of reasoning. After all, this is a storybook.

Therefore, some things are not covered herein even though they are necessary in the study of money management. For example, dependency is an integral element in the study of these concepts, and I recommend some of the earlier books I have written on this subject (Vince 1990, 2007) to learn about dependency.

Some other concepts are not covered but could be, even though they are not necessary to the study of money management. One such concept is that of normal probability distribution. As mentioned above, I've tried to keep this book free of earlier material that wasn't in the direct line of reasoning that this book follows. With other material, such as applying the optimal f notion to other probability distributions (because the ideas herein are applicable to non–market-related concepts of geometric growth functions in general), I've tried to maintain a market-specific theme.

Furthermore, some concepts are often viewed as too abstract, and so I am trying to make their applicability empirically related, for instance, by using discrete, empirically derived distributions in lieu of parametric ones pertaining to price (since, as mentioned earlier, the distributions of trading outcomes are merely the distributions of prices themselves, altered by the trading rules). The world we must exist in, down here on the shop floor of planet earth, is so often *not* characterized by normal distributions or systems of linear equations.

One major notion I have tried to weave throughout the text is that of walk-through examples, particularly in Chapters 4, 5, and 7, covering the more involved algorithms. In these portions of the text, I have tried to provide tables replete with variate values at different steps in the calculations, so that the reader can see exactly what needs to be performed and how to do it. I am a programmer by profession, and I have constructed these examples with an eye toward using them to debug attempted implementations of the material.

Where math is presented within the text, I have tried to keep it simple, straightforward, almost conciliatory in tone. I am not trying to razzle-dazzle here; I am not interested in trying to create *Un Cirque du Soleil Mathématique*. Rather, I am seeking as broad an audience for my concepts as possible (hence the presentation via books, as opposed to arcane journals, and where the reader must do more than merely scour a free web page) in as accessible a manner as possible. My audience, I hope, is the person on the commuter train en route home from the financial district in any major city on the planet. I hope that this reader will see and sense, innately, what I will articulate here. If you, Dear Reader, happen to be a member of the world of academia, please keep this in mind and judge me gently.

Often throughout this text the reader may notice that certain mathematical expressions have been left in unsimplified form, particularly certain rational expressions in later chapters. This is by intent so as to facilitate the ability of the reader to "see" innately what is being discussed, and how the equations in question arise. Hence, clarity trumps mathematical elegance here.

Finally, though the math is presented within the text, the reader may elect not to get involved with the mathematics. I have presented the text in a manner of two congruent, simultaneous channels, with math and without. This is, after all, a story about mathematical concepts. The math is included to buttress the concepts discussed but is not necessary to enjoy the story.

PART I

The Single Component Case

Optimal f

CHAPTER 1

The General History of Geometric Mean Maximization

G eometric mean maximization, or "growth-optimality," is the idea of maximizing the size of a stake when the amount you have to wager is a function of the outcome of the wagers up to that point. You are trying to maximize the value of a stake over a series of plays wherein you do not add or remove amounts from the stake.

The lineage of reasoning of geometric mean maximization is crucial, for it is important to know how we got here. I will illustrate, in broad strokes, the history of geometric mean maximization because this story is about to take a very sharp turn in Part III, in the reasoning of how we utilize geometric mean maximization. To this point in time, the notion of geometric mean maximization has been a *criterion* (just as being at the growth-optimal point, maximizing growth, has been the criterion before we examine the nature of the curve itself).

We will see later in this text that it is, instead, a framework (something much greater than the antiquated notion of "portfolio models"). This is an unavoidable perspective that gives *context* to our actions, but our criterion is rarely growth optimality. Yet growth optimality is the criterion that is solved mathematically. Mathematics, devoid of human propensities, proclivities, and predilections, can readily arrive at a clean, "optimal" point. As such, it provides a framework for us to satisfy our seemingly labyrinthine appetites.

On the ninth of September 1713, Swiss mathematician Nicolaus Bernoulli, whose fascination with difference equations had him corresponding with French mathematician Pierre Raymond de Montmort, whose fascination was finite differences, wrote to Montmort about a paradox that involved the intersection of their interests.

Bernoulli described a game of heads and tails, a coin toss in which you essentially pay a cover charge to play. A coin is tossed. If the coin comes up heads, it is tossed again repeatedly until it comes up tails. The pot starts at one unit and doubles every time the coin comes up heads. You win whatever is in the pot when the game ends. So, if you win on the first toss, you get your one unit back. If tails doesn't appear until the second toss, you get two units back. On the third toss, a tails will get you four units back, *ad infinitum*.

Thus, you win 2^{q-1} units if tails appears on the qth toss.

The question is "What *should* you pay to enter this game, in order for it to be a 'fair' game based on Mathematical Expectation?"

Suppose you win one unit with probability .5, two units with probability .25, four units with probability .125, *ad infinitum*. The Mathematical Expectation is therefore:

$$ME = 2^0 * \frac{1}{2^1} + 2^1 * \frac{1}{2^2} + 2^2 * \frac{1}{2^3} \cdots \qquad (1.01)$$

$$ME = .5 + .5 + .5 \ldots$$

$$ME = \sum_{q=1}^{\infty} .5 = \infty$$

The expected result for a player in such a game is to win an infinite amount. So just what is a fair cover charge, then, to enter such a game?[1] This is quite the paradox indeed, and one that shall rendezvous with us in the sequel in Part III.

The cognates of geometric mean maximization begin with Nicolaus Bernoulli's cousin, Daniel Bernoulli.[2,3] In 1738, 18 years before the birth

---

[1]A cover charge would be consistent with the human experience here. After all, it takes money to make money (though, it doesn't take money to lose money).

[2]Daniel was one of eight members of this family of at least eight famous mathematicians of the late seventeenth through the late eighteenth century. Daniel was cousin to Nicolaus, referred to here, whose father and grandfather bore the same name. The grandson, Daniel's cousin, is often referred to Nicolaus I, and as the nephew of Jakob and Johann Bernoulli, the latter being Daniel's father. As an aside, one of Daniel's two brothers was also named Nicolaus, and he is known as Nicolaus II, who would thus be cousin as well to Nicolaus I, whose father was named Nicolaus as well as his grandfather (the grandfather thus to not only Nicolaus I, but to Daniel and his brothers, including Nicolaus II).

[3]Though in our context we look upon Daniel Bernoulli in the context of his pioneering work in probability, he is primarily famous for his applications of mathematics

of Mozart, Daniel made the first known reference to what is known as "geometric mean maximization." Arguably, his paper drew upon the thoughts and intellectual backdrop of his era, the Enlightenment, the Age of Reason. Although we may credit Daniel Bernoulli here as the first cognate of geometric mean maximization (as he is similarly credited as the father of utility theory by the very same work), he, too, was a product of his time. The incubator for his ideas began in the 1600s in the belching mathematical cauldron of the era.

Prior to that time, there is no known mention in any language of even generalized optimal reinvestment strategies. Merchants and traders, in any of the developing parts of the earth, evidently never formally codified the concept. If it was contemplated by anyone, it was not recorded.

As for what we know of Bernoulli's 1738 paper (originally published in Latin), according to Bernstein (1996), we find a German translation appearing in 1896, and we find a reference to it in John Maynard Keynes' 1921 *Treatise on Probability*.

In 1936, we find an article in *The Quarterly Journal of Economics* called "Speculation and the carryover" by John Burr Williams that pertained to trading in cotton. Williams posited that one should bet on a representative price and that if profits and losses are reinvested, the method of calculating this price is to select the geometric mean of all of the possible prices.

Interesting stuff.

By 1954, we find Daniel Bernoulli's 1738 paper finally translated into English in *Econometrica*.

When so-called game theory came along in the 1950s, concepts were being widely examined by numerous economists, mathematicians, and academicians, and this fecund backdrop is where we find, in 1956, John L. Kelly Jr.'s paper, "A new interpretation of information rate." Kelly demonstrated therein that to achieve maximum wealth, a gambler should maximize the expected value of the logarithm of his capital. This is so because the logarithm is additive in repeated bets and to which the law of large numbers applies. (Maximizing the sum of the logs is akin to maximizing the product of holding period returns, that is, the "Terminal Wealth Relative.")

In his 1956 paper in the *Bell System Technical Journal*, Kelly showed how Shannon's "Information Theory" (Shannon 1948) could be applied to the problem of a gambler who has inside information in determining his growth-optimal bet size.

When one seeks to maximize the expected value of the stake after n trials, one is said to be employing "The Kelly criterion."

---

to mechanics and in particular to fluid mechanics, particularly for his most famous work, *Hydrodynamique* (1738), which was published the very year of the paper of his we are referring to here!

The Kelly criterion states that we should bet that fixed fraction of our stake (f) that maximizes the growth function G(f):

$$G(f) = P * \ln(1 + B * f) + (1 - P) * \ln(1 - f) \qquad (1.02)$$

where: f = the optimal fixed fraction
          P = the probability of a winning bet/trade
          B = the ratio of amount won on a winning bet to amount lost on
              a losing bet
          $\ln(\ )$ = the natural logarithm function

Betting on a fixed fractional basis such as that which satisfies the Kelly criterion is a type of wagering known as a Markov betting system. These are types of betting systems wherein the quantity wagered is not a function of the previous history, but rather, depends only upon the parameters of the wager at hand.

If we satisfy the Kelly criterion, we will be growth optimal in the long-run sense. That is, we will have found an optimal value for f (as the optimal f is the value for f that satisfies the Kelly criterion).

In the following decades, there was an efflorescence of papers that pertained to this concept, and the idea began to embed itself into the world of capital markets, at least in terms of academic discourse, and these ideas were put forth by numerous researchers, notably Bellman and Kalaba (1957), Breiman (1961), Latane (1959), Latane and Tuttle (1967), and many others.

Edward O. Thorp, a colleague of Claude Shannon, and whose work deserves particular mention in this discussion, is perhaps best known for his 1962 book, *Beat the Dealer* (proving blackjack *could* be beaten). In 1966, Thorp developed a winning strategy for side bets in baccarat that employed the Kelly criterion. Thorp has presented formulas to determine the value for f that satisfies the Kelly criterion.

Specifically:

If the amount won is equal to the amount lost:

$$f = 2 * P - 1 \qquad (1.03)$$

which can also be expressed as:

$$f = P - Q \qquad (1.03a)$$

where: f = the optimal fixed fraction
          P = the probability of a winning bet/trade
          Q = The probability of a loss, or the complement of P, equal to 1
              $- P$

Both forms of the equation are equivalent

This will yield the correct answer for the optimal f value provided the quantities are the same regardless of whether a win or a loss. As an example, consider the following stream of bets:

$$-1, +1, +1, -1, -1, +1, +1, +1, +1, -1$$

There are 10 bets, 6 winners, hence:

$$f = 2 * .6 - 1$$
$$= 1.2 - 1$$
$$= .2$$

If all of the winners and losers were not for the same size, then this formula would not yield the correct answer. Reconsider our 2:1 coin toss example wherein we toss a coin and if heads comes up, we win two units and if tails we lose one unit. For such situations the Kelly formula is:

$$f = ((B + 1) * P - 1)/B \qquad (1.04)$$

where: f = the optimal fixed fraction
P = the probability of a winning bet/trade
B = the ratio of amount won on a winning bet to amount lost on a losing bet

In our 2:1 coin toss example:

$$f = ((2 + 1).5 - 1)/2$$
$$= (3 * .5 - 1)/2$$
$$= (1.5 - 1)/2$$
$$= .5/2$$
$$= .25$$

This formula yields the correct answer for optimal f provided all wins are always for the same amount and all losses are always for the same amount (that is, most gambling situations). If this is not so, then this formula does *not* yield the correct answer.

Notice that the numerator in this formula equals the Mathematical Expectation for an event with two possible outcomes. Therefore, we can say that as long as all wins are for the same amount, and all losses are for the same amount (regardless of whether the amount that can be won equals the amount that can be lost), the f that is optimal is:

$$f = \text{Mathematical Expectation}/B \qquad (1.05)$$

The concept of geometric mean maximization did not go unchallenged in subsequent decades. Notables such as Samuelson (1971, 1979), Goldman (1974), Merton and Samuelson (1972), and others posited various and compelling arguments to not accept geometric mean maximization as the criterion for investors.

By the late 1950s and in subsequent decades there was a different, albeit similar, discussion that is separate and apart from geometric mean maximization. This is the discussion of portfolio optimization. This parallel line of reasoning, that of maximizing returns vis-à-vis "risk," absent the effects of reinvestment, would gain widespread acceptance in the financial community and relegate geometric mean maximization to the back seat in the coming decades, in terms of a tool for relative allocations.

Markowitz's 1952 *Portfolio Selection* laid the foundations for what would become known as "Modern Portfolio Theory." A host of others, such as William Sharpe, added to the collective knowledge of this burgeoning discipline.

Apart from geometric mean maximization, there were points of overlap. In 1969 Thorp presented the notion that the Kelly criterion should replace the Markowitz criterion in portfolio selection. By 1971 Thorp had applied the Kelly criterion to portfolio selection. In 1976, Markowitz too would join in the debate of geometric growth optimization. I illustrated how the notions of Modern Portfolio Theory and Geometric Mean Optimization could overlap in 1992 via the Pythagorean relationship of the arithmetic returns and the standard deviation in those returns.

The reason that this similar, overlapping discussion of Modern Portfolio Theory is presented is because it *has* seen such widespread acceptance. Yet, according to Thorp, as well as this author (Vince 1995, 2007), it is trumped by geometric mean maximization in terms of portfolio selection.

It was Thorp who presented the "Kelly Formulas," which satisfy the Kelly criterion (which "seeks to maximize the expected value of the stake after n trials"). This was first presented in the context of two possible gambling outcomes, a winning outcome and a losing outcome. Understand that the Kelly formulas presented by Thorp caught hold, and people were trying to implement them in the trading community.

In 1983, Fred Gehm referred to the notion of using Thorp's Kelly Formulas, and pointed out they are only applicable when the probability of a win, the amount won and the amount lost, "completely describe the distribution of potential profits and losses." Gehm concedes that "this is not the case" (in trading). Gehm's book, *Commodity Market Money Management*, was written in 1983, and thus he concluded (regarding determining the optimal fraction to bet in trading) "there is no alternative except to use complicated and expensive Monte Carlo techniques." (Gehm 1983, p. 108)

In 1987, the Pension Research Institute at San Francisco State University put forth some mathematical algorithms to amend the concepts of Modern Portfolio Theory to account for the differing sentiments investors had pertaining to upside variance versus downside variance. This approach was coined "Postmodern Portfolio Theory."

The list of names in this story of mathematical twists and turns is nowhere near complete. There were many others in the past three centuries, particularly in recent decades, who added much to this discussion, whose names are not even mentioned here.

I am not seeking to interject myself among these august names. Rather, I am trying to show the lineage of reasoning that leads to the ideas presented in this book, which necessarily requires the addition of ideas I have previously written about. As I said, a very sharp turn is about to occur for two notions—the notion of geometric mean maximization as a criterion, and the notion of the value of "portfolio models." Those seemingly parallel lines of thought are about to change.

In September 2007, I gave a talk in Stockholm on the Leverage Space Model, the maximization for multiple, simultaneous positions, and juxtaposed it to a quantification of the probability of a given drawdown. Near the end of the talk, one supercilious character snidely asked, "So what's new? I don't see anything new in what you've presented." Without accusing me outright, he seemed to imply that I was presenting, in effect, Kelly's 1956 paper with a certain elision toward it.

This has been furtively volleyed up to me on more than one occasion: the intimation that I somehow repackaged the Kelly paper and, further, that what I have presented was already presented in Kelly. Those who believe this are conflating Kelly's paper with what I have written, and they are often ignorant of just what the Kelly paper does contain, and where it first appears.

In fact, I have tried to use the same mathematical nomenclature as Thorp, Kelly, and others, including the use of "f" and "G"[4] solely to provide continuity for those who want the full story, how it connects, and out of

---

[4]In this text, however, we will refer to the geometric mean HPR as GHPR, as opposed to G, which is how I, as well as the others, have previously referred to it. I am using this nomenclature to be consistent with the variable we will be referring to later, AHPR, as the arithmetic mean HPR.

respect for these pioneering, soaring minds. I have not claimed to be the eponym for anything I have uncovered or added to this discussion.

Whether known by Kelly or not, the cognates to his paper are from Daniel Bernoulli. It is very likely that Bernoulli was not the originator of the idea, either. In fairness to Kelly, the paper was presented as a solution to a technological problem that did not exist in Daniel Bernoulli's day.

As for the Kelly paper, it merely tells us, for at least the second time, that there is an optimal fraction in terms of quantity when what we have to work with on subsequent periods is a function of what happens during this period.

Yes, the idea is monumental. Its application, I found, left me with a great deal of work to be done. Fortunately, the predecessors in this nearly three-centuries-old story to these lines of thought memorialized what they had seen, what they found to be true about it.

I was introduced to the notion of geometric mean maximization by Larry Williams, who showed me Thorp's "Kelly Formulas," which he sought to apply to the markets (because he has the nerve for it).

Seeing that this was no mere nostrum and that there was some inherent problem with it (in applying those formulas to the markets, as they mathematically solve for a "2 possible outcome" gambling situation), I sought a means of applying the concept to a stream of trades. Nothing up to that point provided me with the tools to do so. Yes, it is geometric mean maximization, or "maximizing the sum of the logs," but it's not in a gambling situation. If I followed that path without amendment, I would end up with a "number" between 0 and X. It tells me neither what my "risk" is (as a percentage of account equity) nor how many contracts or shares to put on.

Because I wanted to apply the concept of geometric mean maximization to trading, I had to discern my own formulas, because this was not a gambling situation (nor was it bound between 0 and 1), to represent the fraction of our stake at risk, just as the gambling situation innately bounds f between 0 and 1.

In 1990, I provided my equations to do just that. To find the optimal f (for "fraction," thus implying a number $0 <= f <= 1$), given a stream of trades (or, of periodic profits and losses; for example, the daily, or monthly, or quarterly, or annual profit/loss), we must first convert them into a "Holding Period Return," remaining within the nomenclature of those before me, for a given f value, or "HPR(f)." This is simply $1 +$ the rate of return, and is given as:

$$HPR(f) = 1 + f * \frac{-trade}{BiggestLoss} \qquad (1.06)$$

where: f = the value we are using for f
$-trade$ = the profit or loss on a trade with the sign reversed so that losses are positive numbers and profits are negative
$BiggestLoss$ = the P&L over the entire stream that resulted in the biggest loss. (This should always be a negative number.)

Thus, a gain of 5 percent would see an HPR(f) of 1.05. A loss of 5 percent would see an HPR(f) of .95.

By multiplying together all of the HPR(f)s, we obtain the "Terminal Wealth Relative," or "TWR(f)." This is simply the geometric product of the HPR(f)s, and it represents the multiple made on our starting stake at the end of the stream of profits and losses:

$$TWR(f) = \prod_{i=1}^{n} HPR(f)_i \qquad (1.07)$$

or:

$$TWR(f) = \prod_{i=1}^{n} \left(1 + f * \frac{-trade_i}{BiggestLoss}\right) \qquad (1.07a)$$

and geometric mean (GHPR(f)) is simply the nth root of the TWR(f). GHPR(f) represents the multiple you made on your stake, on average, per HPR(f):

$$GHPR(f) = \sqrt[n]{\prod_{i=1}^{n} HPR(f)_i} = \left(\prod_{i=1}^{n} HPR(f)_i\right)^{1/n} \qquad (1.08)$$

or:

$$GHPR(f) = \sqrt[n]{\prod_{i=1}^{n} \left(1 + f * \frac{-trade_i}{BiggestLoss}\right)}$$

$$= \left(\prod_{i=1}^{n} \left(1 + f * \frac{-trade_i}{BiggestLoss}\right)\right)^{1/n} \qquad (1.08a)$$

where: f = the value we are using for f

$-trade_i$ = the profit or loss on the ith trade with the sign reversed so that losses are positive numbers and profits are negative

$BiggestLoss$ = the P&L that resulted in the biggest loss. (This should always be a negative number.)

n = the total number of trades

$GHPR(f)$ = the geometric mean of the $HPR(f)$s

The value for $f (0 <= f <= 1)$ that maximizes $GHPR(f)$ (or $TWR(f)$, as both are maximized at the same value for f) is the optimal f. It is an optimization problem: Simply optimize f for greatest $GHPR(f)$ or $TWR(f)$. The value for the optimal f is irrespective of the order the $HPR(f)$s occur in; all permutations of a stream of $HPR(f)$s result in the same optimal f value.

These equations would give you the same answer for the 2:1 coin toss as the Kelly formula answer of $f = .25$. So, these formulas can be used in lieu of the Kelly formulas. What's more, these formulas work when there are more than two possible outcomes.

Furthermore, the f derived from the 1990 procedure detailed here can then be converted into a number of "units" to put on (number of shares or contracts). Since the inputs in terms of $trade_i$ and biggest loss must be determined from a particular trading size, be it 100 shares or one contract, it can be any arbitrary, though consistent, amount you choose (which we will call a "unit"). Thus, once an optimal f is determined, based on the results of trading in one unit, we can determine how many units we should have on for a given trade or period (depending upon whether the stream of $HPR(f)$s was derived by using trades or periods) as:

$$f\$ = -BiggestLoss/f \qquad\qquad (1.09)$$

$f\$$ represents how much to capitalize each unit for a given trade or period by. To then determine how many units to have on:

$$\text{Number of Units to Assume} = \text{Account Equity}/f\$ \qquad (1.10)$$

For example, if we have a stake of 100 units, a biggest loss of -1 units (using our 2:1 coin toss game here) and an f of .25, we would thus have:

$$f\$ = -BiggestLoss/f$$

$$f\$ = -(-1)/.25$$

$$f\$ = 1/.25$$

$$f\$ = 4$$

(So, if one unit is one wager in this game, we make one wager for every 4 units in our stake):

$$\text{Number of Units to Assume} = 100/4 = 25$$

Thus, we make 25 wagers, which in this case correspond to a 25 percent fraction of our stake risked.

If we were trading and we had an optimal $f\$$ of .25, and our biggest loss per unit was 10,000 units, we would have an $f\$$ of 40,000 units and would thus trade one unit per every 40,000 units in our account equity. Such a position sizing would represent having 25 percent of our account at risk.

Do not be dissuaded by margin requirements. They have nothing to do with what is the mathematically optimal amount to finance a trade by (often, margin requirements will be more than $f\$$).

Do not be dissuaded by having the variable *BiggestLoss* in the equations. This will be addressed in the following chapter.

So these equations can be used in lieu of the Kelly formulas for trading situations, but they are applicable to trading only one game, only one component, at a given time.

However, I was interested in multiple, simultaneous games that were not simply gambling games. I was interested in portfolios of tradable components and thus had to determine my own equations for dealing with multiple, simultaneous positions, because again, this is a trading situation. Kelly and others intimated that such an approach could be worked out for trading, and in my search for answers to these problems I had encountered Mike Pascual, a brilliant fellow, who had worked it out for gambling situations (taking the Kelly Formulas to the next level—multiple, simultaneous wagers). Yet even so I was left in a dead end in terms of applying this approach to market outcomes for the very same reasons that I could not apply the Kelly Formulas to market outcomes of a single component; the distribution of market outcomes is more complex than for gambling outcomes. (I will not attempt to cover all that Pascual has covered; interested readers are referred to Pascual [1987]).

I had to work out the formulas for geometric mean maximization for market-related situations (and bounding the result, f, between 0 and 1) as opposed to simpler, gambling illustrations, and I had to work it out for multiple, simultaneous "plays," that is, "portfolios." The equations for such will be provided later in this story, when we get to the discussion of Leverage Space Part II.

Most important, where the predecessors (including Kelly) of this "geometric mean maximization" notion came up short for me, in terms of market application, was that they only alluded to the fact that there *was* an optimal point.

Having an optimal point implies a curved function, and it is the dynamics of the curve itself (as bound between 0 and 1, to put in context and give meaning to being on the curve!) that we use to discern the information about our actions in the marketplace. There are a great deal of information, payoffs, and consequences to being at different points along this curve (which, because we are oblivious to them, we are likely migrating along with each trade, and hence, assuming different potential payoffs and consequences from trade to trade!).

Furthermore, as I pursued my passion in this vein, I discovered what really was an entire domain to this netherworld that had been heretofore undiscovered: the very nature of the curve. Prior to my illumination of the character of these curves (and the fact that they are at work on us whether we acknowledge them or not), people, very smart guys in fact, would talk about things like betting "half Kelly," or other arbitrary, ad hoc things like this. I could see that no one had explored the dynamics of the curve. That is where the real story is here. (Because "half kelly" is an arbitrary point in terms of the dynamics of the curve and shows a common perspective that is oblivious to the dynamics of the curve, and hence, the tradeoffs of the curve and the mathematically significant points moving and migrating along it.)

It is the character of the curve whereupon the optimal point resides that *is* what is the netherworld, it *is* leverage space. The nature of the curve itself—that *is* where we find information about our actions, and therefore what we shall discuss in forthcoming chapters.

I had unwittingly stumbled into what was an entire domain, found myself in a place alive with geometric relationships, this place I call this netherworld of "leverage space." Things, the good predecessors in this line of reasoning evidently never saw, which I have had the pleasure of being utterly fascinated by.

Had others in this nearly three-centuries-old story seen this, they would have memorialized in writing what they had seen regarding these things, as I have tried to do over the decades.

I contend you are somewhere on the curve, ineluctably, and that there are characteristics to being at different points on that curve that have not been identified. Further, unless you are risking a certain, fixed, percentage of your "stake" on each "play," you are ineluctably migrating about that curve, and the characteristics of those heretofore-unidentified points on that curve apply to you, but unbeknownst to you.

CHAPTER 2

The Ineluctable Coordinates

To start with, we can pinpoint your location in this unknown nether-world of quantity with respect to a single, tradable instrument (which for the single component case consists of a single curve in a two-dimensional plane) by the variable f, as that is how it has been referred to previously in the literature.

Everyone, on every trade, on every opportunity involving risk, has an f value whether they acknowledge it or not. And we can determine your assigned f value for any tradable instrument at any point in time as follows:

$$f = |\text{BiggestLoss}|/f\$ \qquad (2.01)$$

where:

$$f\$ = \text{Account Equity/Units} \qquad (2.02)$$

(Recall that $f\$$ represents how much capitalization is behind each position.)

We can also state, as we have in the previous chapter, that:

$$f\$ = |\text{BiggestLoss}|/f \qquad (1.09)$$

And again, a unit is a standard size, whatever you want it to be—for instance, 100 shares, one futures or options contract, ten million USD in forex, and so on.

Example:

One unit will be 100 shares. Assume we have 2 units, 200 shares.
$50,000 account
Biggest Losing Outcome for One Unit is −$10,000

So:

$$f\$ = 50,000/2 = 25,000$$

Thus:

$$f = |-10,000|/25,000 = .4$$

From this, then, we can state that your f value, your location in leverage space, is .4.

Ah, there it is: Biggest Loss. I hear your protests already.

But you *do* know your biggest loss. It is that amount that answers the question "What's the absolute worst thing that can happen here?" without regard to what the probability of that might be, short of the world suddenly ending. Now, if you cannot answer that, it is *still* not a problem, and there *are* solutions, as we will see momentarily.

So we can state that everyone, on every trade, has an "f value" that can be assigned to them, a number (a "location," a "coordinate") between 0 and 1, ineluctably, whether they acknowledge this or not.

And the reason is that all of the inputs to determine that f value are givens: quantity put on, biggest perceived losing outcome, and account equity.

Lastly, don't confuse the f value you ineluctably have with what is the optimal f value. You may be at the optimal f value. Regardless, you are at some f value, though it most likely is not the optimal value for f (in terms of maximizing geometric growth).

Let's take a tradable instrument, such as a bond priced at 60 today, and consider what the future might hold. We can say that there is a cone that goes into the future of possible outcomes. Actually, the cone is bell-shaped on all three axes, comporting with the notion of volatility changing with the square of time (on the X-axis), as well as the pareto-like nature of price changes (where the cone flares, into a bell-like shape, on the Y- and Z-axes.) See Figure 2.1.

Along the bell-shaped cone in three axes, we can look at the discrete snapshots in time (which run along the X-axis) and derive pareto-like distributions at those X values, those discrete points in time. See Figure 2.2.

Remember, along the trajectory, not only the trajectory (which represents the mode of the probabilities functions along it) but also the

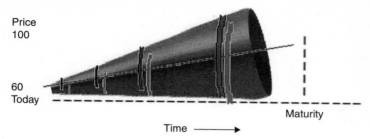

FIGURE 2.1 Trajectory Cone (Bell-Shaped on All 3 Axes)

probability functions themselves are affected by possible call or put provisions, coupon dates, and so on. In real life, it is not as smooth as depicted in Figure 2.2.

Essentially, we take continuous distributions of what can happen and convert these to binned distributions. We'll call each bin a "scenario," where each scenario has an outcome (A) and an associated probability (P). See Figure 2.3.

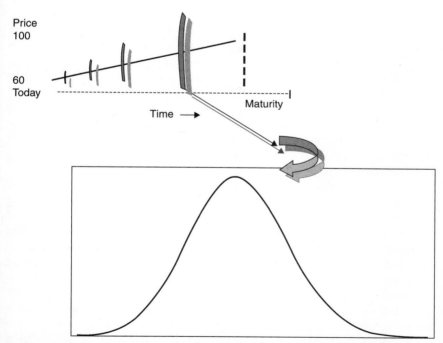

FIGURE 2.2 At Snapshots in Time, There Is a Distribution About the Trajectory

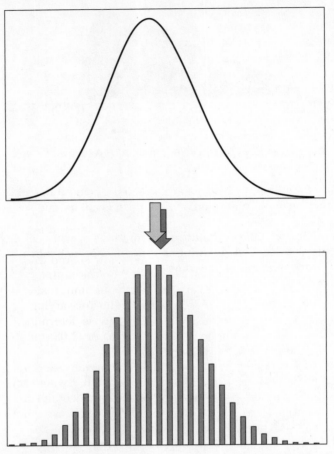

FIGURE 2.3 The Distribution Can Be Made into Bins (a Scenario Is a Bin with a Probability and an Outcome)

The biggest losing outcome is that of the leftmost scenario. Yes, the tails on the left continue on into negative infinity in many cases (not the lognormal, by the way), but one of the fundamental questions regarding decisions of any type is always "What's the worst thing that I think can happen?"

Sometimes this is not so difficult. "Hey, I'm long 100 shares at 100 a share. My biggest losing outcome is 10,000."

Similarly if I am buying time premium in options, my biggest loss is truncated, and other such left-tail-truncation vehicles exist.

In other cases, absent such left-tail-truncation vehicles (or outright long positions where the lognormal distribution truncates our biggest loss), we select a worst case to budget for.

Finally, if you still cannot answer the question of "what's the worst thing that can happen?" it still does not mean you are not in the netherworld of leverage space. It simply means that we're having a hard time locating you down there, that's all. Even that does not negate your having ineluctable coordinates—only the coordinate system's range.

The most important thing about defining a worst case scenario is to *not* get hung up on it. *It is required solely to bind the f value between 0 and 1.*

In Chapter 1 we discussed our 2:1 coin toss example, and showed how the optimal f for such a game is .25. Since the largest loss is -1, dividing the absolute value of this by .25 yields an $f\$$ of 4$ ($|-1|/.25 = 4$), or make one bet for every \$4 in our stake. Now, if we arbitrarily say that our Biggest-Loss parameter is \$2 (leaving both scenarios the same, a loss of \$1 and a gain of \$2, but using a new BiggestLoss parameter of \$2 to (1.06) or (1.07a) or (1.08a)) we find that our optimal f value is now .5. And we subsequently divide the absolute value of our largest loss by the optimal f value, and obtain an $f\$$ of $|-2|/.5 = 4$. Again, we trade one unit, make one bet, for every \$4 in our stake. Table 2.1 demonstrates this for varying values of our biggest loss, wherein the optimal f, for each row, is determined using that row's BiggestLoss in equations (1.06) or (1.07a) or (1.08a) in determining the optimal f at that row.

Unlike the gambling situations, which the predecessors of geometric mean maximization were primarily concerned with, I wanted to tie in the similar notion here that you are risking f% of your account equity. In other words, *if* the biggest losing outcome manifests itself, we will lose f% of the account at that time. That's all. People look for reasons to categorically dismiss this, but don't do it based on the fact that I incorporate the worst perceived loss *a priori*.

You see, we could use an arbitrary value in lieu of biggest loss, pump it through the formulas, and guess what? For a given level of account

TABLE 2.1 $f\$$ and GHPR Invariant to Biggest Loss

BiggestLoss	f	f$	GHPR
−0.6	.15	4	1.125
−1	.25	4	1.125
−2	.5	4	1.125
−5	1.25	4	1.125
−29	7.25	4	1.125

equity, you would optimally *still* trade the same number of units! Biggest loss does *not* affect the final answers here. I incorporate it simply to bound f between 0 and 1, so that it represents a percentage of your entire account that is at risk, and so that it puts things on an apples-to-apples basis with the predecessors who discussed geometric mean maximization in gambling situations.

You can forget about margin, because that has nothing to do with the optimal fraction of the stake to bet or the optimal fraction of an account at risk. It has nothing to do with your leverage. From this point on, think of "leverage" in terms of an f value. The conventional notion of leverage is one that only warns, "Be careful, you're taking on a lot of risk."

From now on, you will think of leverage as a number between 0 and 1, a number that, if the worst case scenario does manifest, is the percentage of account equity you lose. You see, f is your measure of leverage, whether you've borrowed money to carry the position or not.

Here's what you're doing in your technical analysis in effect: determining a positive *mode*—the single most likely outcome or "scenario"—to this distribution. You may also be determining "confidence intervals," on the left and right, that is, targets, projections, stop losses, and so on.

However, even at that, are you using the probabilities of that information in a manner that gives you an indication of how much quantity to have on for an account? That is what we are going to do. We are going to use these binned distributions (at a given point in time, that is, at a particular point along the trajectory cone), their bins, their "scenarios" as I call them, which are a probability of something happening (the vertical height of the bin, "P") and the associated payoff or loss to it happening (the horizontal location of the bin, "A") to determine the optimal fraction to bet.

Let's look at a simplified distribution. Often, we can use gambling situations as a proxy for market situations because gambling illustrations tend to be considerably simpler (fewer scenarios and therefore simpler distributions). The mathematics is the same except that market probabilities seem to be "chronomorphic," that is, they change with time.

Let's again consider our 2:1 coin toss example. Essentially, to figure the Mathematical Expectation of a binned distribution, we take the sum of each bin's outcome times its probability (Figure 2.4).

Here is our binned distribution—our scenario spectrum—and here are its scenarios. Note that each scenario has a probability, P, associated with it (.5 each) and an associated outcome, A (-1 and $+2$).

Which brings us back to the notion of Mathematical Expectation, or "Expected Value." In this case, the same formula given in the introduction for Mathematical Expectation is used to determine the expected

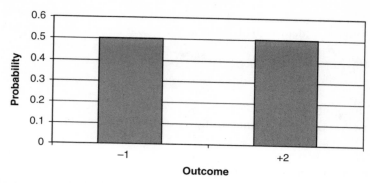

FIGURE 2.4 2:1 Coin Toss Probability Outcome

value of the entire binned distribution, of the scenario spectrum:

$$ME = \sum_{i=1}^{n} (P_i * A_i)$$

where: P_i = the probability associated with the ith scenario
A_i = the result of the ith scenario
n = the total number of scenarios under consideration

Essentially, to figure the Mathematical Expectation of a binned distribution, we take the sum of each bin's outcome times its probability.

Mathematical expectation is what we expect to make, on average, on a given play.

In our 2:1 coin toss the ME is .5 units per play $(-1 * .5 + 2 * .5 = -.5 + 1 = .5)$. But what if we are wagering only a fraction of our entire stake?

As mentioned earlier, for any scenario spectrum, any binned distribution, we have an f value. In this case, the 2:1 coin toss:

- Assume a 10 unit stake.
- Worst-Case Outcome −1 unit.
- We are wagering five units.
- Thus, $f\$ = 10/5 = 2$ (one bet for every two units in our stake).
- Thus $f = |-1|/2 = .5$.
- Thus, when the biggest loss manifests, we lose f percent of our stake—50 percent in this case.

You might be saying, "Okay, I have an f value, a value between 0 and 1, but so what?"

CHAPTER 3

The Nature of the Curve

I n a game such as our 2:1 coin toss, Figure 3.1 shows what people would *think* they make, based on various levels of leverage.

The vertical axis in Figure 3.1 represents the multiple on their stake with respect to the horizontal axis, which represents the fraction of their stake risked.

The function, the line in Figure 3.1, is simply $1 + ME/|BL| * f$ (where f is the fraction of your stake you are putting at risk. Thus, at 1.0 you would expect a 1.5 multiple on your stake, given a .5 Mathematical Expectation).

People think this is a straight-line function, and in a "one-shot-sense," it is.

But the "one-shot-sense" is merely fiction. Here's why.

People trade/bet in ways that are relative to the size of their stake or account. (You wouldn't trade a $5,000,000 account the same as a $50,000 one, would you? If an account went from, say, $100,000 to $500,000, would you trade in the same quantity? What if it went the other way around?) It happens to be a fortunate fact that an account grows fastest when traded in size relative to the size of the account.

Most traders gloss over this decision about quantity. They feel that it is somewhat arbitrary in that it doesn't much matter what quantity they have on. What matters is that they be right about the direction of the trade, that is, that the *mode* of the distribution, the single most likely bin, be > 0.

Notice that if we have only one play, we maximize growth by maximizing the arithmetic average holding period return AHPR(f), (that is, $f = 1$). If we have an infinite number of plays, we maximize growth by maximizing the geometric average holding period return GHPR(f), (that

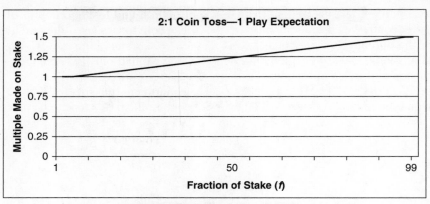

Multiple made on stake = 1 + ME/|BL| * f
(a.k.a. Holding Period Return, HPR)

FIGURE 3.1 The Mistaken Impression

is, f = optimal f). However, *the f that is truly optimal is a function of the length of time—the number of holding period returns—which we are going to play.*[1]

For one holding period return, the optimal f will always be 1.0 for a positive arithmetic Mathematical Expectation game. If we bet at any value for f other than 1.0, and quit after only one holding period, we will not have maximized our expected average geometric growth. What we regard as the optimal f will be optimal only if you were to play for an infinite number of holding periods. The f that is truly optimal starts at one for a positive arithmetic Mathematical Expectation game, and converges toward what we call the optimal f as the number of holding periods approaches infinity.

To see this, consider again our 2:1 coin toss game where we have determined the optimal f to be .25. So, if the coin tosses are independent of previous tosses, by betting 25 percent of our stake on each and every play we will maximize our geometric growth with certainty as the length of this game, the number of tosses (that is, the number of holding periods, n) approaches infinity. Our expected average geometric growth, then—what we would expect to end up with, as an expected value, given every possible combination of outcomes—would be greatest if we bet 25 percent per play.

Consider the first toss. There is a 50 percent probability of winning two units, and a 50 percent probability of losing one unit. At the second toss, there is a 25 percent chance of winning two units on the first toss and winning two units on the second, a 25 percent chance of winning two units on the first and losing one unit on the second, a 25 percent chance of losing one unit on the first and winning two units on the second, and

---

[1]Note that at $n = 1$, that is, if there is only 1 holding period, AHPR(f) = GHPR(f).

a 25 percent chance of losing one unit on the first and losing one unit on the second (we assume the outcomes of these coin tosses are independent of the outcomes of previous tosses). The combinations bloom out in time in a tree-like fashion as depicted below. Since we had only two scenarios (heads and tails) in this scenario spectrum, there are only two branches off each node in the tree. If we had more scenarios in this spectrum, there would be that many more branches off of each node in this tree:

Toss #1	Toss #2	Toss #3
		Heads
	Heads	
		Tails
Heads		
		Heads
	Tails	
		Tails
		Heads
	Heads	
		Tails
Tails		
		Heads
	Tails	
		Tails

If we bet 25 percent of our stake on the first toss and quit, we will not have maximized our expected average compound growth (EACG).

What if we quit after the second toss? What then optimally should we bet knowing that we maximize our expected average compound gain by betting at $f = 1$ when we are going to quit after one play, and betting at the optimal f if we are going to play for an infinite length of time?

If we go back and optimize f, allowing a different f value to be used for the first play as well as the second play, with the intent of maximizing our average geometric mean HPR at the end of the second play, we would find the following. First, the optimal f for quitting after two plays in this game approaches the asymptotic optimal, going from 1.0 if we quit after one play, to .5 for both the first play and the second. Put another way, if we were to quit after the second play, we should optimally bet .5 on both the first and second plays to maximize growth. (Remember that we allowed for the first play to be an f value different from the second, yet they both came out the same, .5 in this case. It is a fact that if you are looking to maximize growth, the f that is optimal, for finite as well as infinite streams, is uniform.)

We can see this if we take the first two possible combinations of tosses:

Toss #1	Toss #2
	Heads
Heads	
	Tails
	Heads
Tails	
	Tails

This can be represented by the following outcomes:

Toss #1	Toss #2
	2
2	
	-1
	2
-1	
	-1

These outcomes can be expressed as holding period returns, for various f values. In the following it is shown for an f of .5 for the first toss, as well as an f of .5 for the second:

Toss #1	Toss #2
	2
2	
	.5
	2
.5	
	.5

Now we can express all tosses subsequent to the first toss as TWR(f)s by multiplying by the subsequent tosses on the tree. The numbers following the last toss on the tree, the numbers in parentheses, are the last TWR(f)s taken to the root of $1/n$, where n equals the number of holding periods, or tosses, in this case 2, and represent the geometric mean HPR for that terminal node on the tree:

Toss #1	Toss #2	GHPR(.5)
	4	2.0
2		
	1	1.0
	1	1.0
−1		
	.25	0.5

Now if we total up the geometric mean HPRs, and take their arithmetic average, we obtain the *expected average compound growth*, in this case:

$$
\begin{array}{l}
2.0 \\
1.0 \\
1.0 \\
0.5 \\
\hline
4.5 / 4 = 1.125
\end{array}
$$

Thus, if we were to quit after two plays, and yet do this same thing over an infinite number of times (that is, quit after two plays), we would optimally bet .5 of our stake on each and every play, thus maximizing our expected average compound growth (EACG).

Notice that we did not bet with an f of 1.0 on the first play even though that is what would have maximized our expected average compound growth if we quit at one play. Instead, if we are planning on quitting after two plays, we maximize our EACG growth by betting at .5 on both the first play and all subsequent plays.

Notice that the f that is optimal in order to maximize growth is uniform for all plays, yet is a function of how long you will play. If you are to quit after only one play, the f that is optimal is the f that maximizes the arithmetic mean HPR (which is always an f of 1.0 for a positive expectation game, 0.0 for a negative expectation game). If you are playing a positive expectation game, the f that is optimal continues to decrease as the length of time at which you quit grows, and, asymptotically, if you play for an infinitely long time, the f that is optimal is that which maximizes the geometric mean HPR. In a negative expectation game, the f that is optimal simply stays at 0.

The f that you use to maximize growth is always uniform. However, that uniform amount is a function of where you intend to quit the game. If you are playing the 2:1 coin toss game, and you intend to quit after one play, you have an f value that provides for optimal growth of 1.0. If you intend to quit after two plays, you have an f that is optimal for maximizing growth of .5 on the first toss, and .5 on the second. Notice, you do not bet 1.0 on the first toss here if you are planning on maximizing the EACG, quitting at the end of the second play. Likewise if you were planning on playing for an infinitely long period of time, you would optimally bet .25 on the first toss and .25 on each subsequent toss.

Note the key word there is *infinitely*, not *indefinitely*. All streams are finite. Each of us will die eventually. As the man in Kentucky says, "It's a mile and a quarter, and that's all they go, the first Saturday in May."

Therefore, when we speak of the optimal f as the f that maximizes expected average compound return, we are speaking of that value that maximizes growth as if we were to play for an infinitely long period of time. Actually, it is slightly suboptimal because none of us will be able to play for an infinitely long time. Actually, the f that will maximize EACG will be slightly above, have us take slightly heavier positions, than what we are calling the optimal f.

What if we were to quit after three tosses? Shouldn't the f then that maximizes expected average compound growth be lower still than the .5 it is at quitting after two plays, yet still be greater than the .25 optimal for an infinitely long game?

Let's examine the tree of combinations here:

Toss #1	Toss #2	Toss #3
		Heads
	Heads	
		Tails
Heads		
		Heads
	Tails	
		Tails
		Heads
	Heads	
		Tails
Tails		
		Heads
	Tails	
		Tails

Converting these to outcomes yields:

Toss #1	Toss #2	Toss #3
		2
	2	
		−1
2		
		2
	−1	
		−1
		2
	2	
		−1
−1		
		2
	−1	
		−1

If I go back with a computer and iterate to that value for f that maximizes expected average compound growth quitting after three tosses, we find it to be .37868. Therefore, if we convert the outcomes to HPRs based upon a .37868 value for f at each toss yields:

Toss #1	Toss #2	Toss #3
		1.757369
	1.757369	
		.621316
1.757369		
		1.757369
	.621316	
		.621316
		1.757369
	1.757369	
		.621316
.621316		
		1.757369
	.621316	
		.621316

Now we can express all tosses subsequent to the first toss as TWR(f)s by multiplying by the subsequent tosses on the tree. The numbers following the last toss on the tree, the numbers in parentheses, are the last TWR(f)s taken to the root of $1/n$, where n equals the number of holding periods, or tosses, in this case 3, and represent the geometric mean HPR for that terminal node on the tree:

Toss #1	Toss #2	Toss #3	GHPR(.37868)
		5.427324	1.757365
	3.088329		
		1.918831	1.242641
1.757369			
		1.918848	1.242644
	1.09188		
		0.678409	0.87868
		1.918824	1.242639
	1.091875		
		0.678401	0.878676
0.621316			
		0.678406	0.878678
	0.386036		
		0.239851	0.621318

$$8.742641 / 8 =$$

1.09283 is the expected average compound growth, the EACG. From this, we can summarize the following conclusions:

1. To maximize the expected average compound growth, EACG, we always end up with a uniform f. The value for f, then, is uniform from one play to the next.

2. The f that is optimal in terms of maximizing the expected average compound growth is a function of the length of the game. For positive expectation games, it starts at 1.0, the value that maximizes the arithmetic mean HPR, diminishes slightly each play, and asymptotically approaches the value that maximizes the geometric mean HPR (which we have been calling, and will continue to call throughout the sequel, the optimal f).

3. Since all streams are finite in length, regardless of how long, we will always be ever so slightly suboptimal by trading at what we call the optimal f, regardless of how long we trade, yet the difference diminishes with each holding period. Ultimately, we are to the left of the peak

TABLE 3.1	Coin Toss Game	
Quitting After HPR#	***f* (which maximizes EACG)**	
1	1.0	
2	.5	
3	.37868	
4	.33626	
5	.3148	
6	.3019	
7	.2932	
8	.2871	
infinity	.25	(this is the value we refer to as the "optimal *f*")

of what was truly optimal. This isn't to say that everything we will be discussing about the $N+1$-dimensional landscape—the penalties and payoffs of where you are with respect to the optimal *f* for each market system—isn't true. It is true. However, the landscape is a function of the number of holding periods at which you quit. The landscapes we project with the techniques in this book are the asymptotic altitudes, what the landscape approaches in the very long run.

To see this, let's continue with our 2:1 coin toss. In Table 3.1, we can see what the value for *f* is that optimally maximizes our expected average compound growth, for quitting at one play through eight plays. Notice how it approaches the optimal *f* of .25, the value that maximizes growth asymptotically as the number of holding periods approaches infinity, as shown in Figure 3.2.

In reality then, if we trade with what we are calling in this text the optimal *f*, we will always be slightly suboptimal, the degree of which diminishes as more and more holding periods elapse. If we knew exactly how many holding periods we were going to trade for, we could then use that value for *f* that maximizes EACG (which would be slightly greater than the optimal *f*) and be truly optimal.[2] Unfortunately, we almost never

---

[2]Thus, the optimal *f* point is never really optimal; the Kelly criterion is never the point that maximizes the growth of capital, except in the abstract case of an infinite number of plays. In a game with a positive Mathematical Expectation, the optimal *f* point is that point that begins at 1.0 (wager the entire stake) if one were looking to play only 1 play. This point, the point that maximizes the growth of capital, migrates from 1.0 in a leftward direction toward the optimal *f* point as the number of plays one is looking to participate in gets ever-greater. It never reaches down

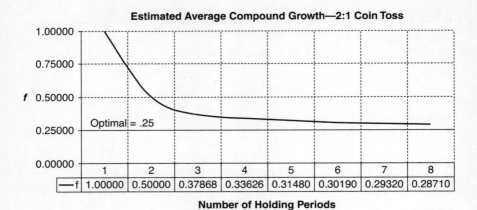

FIGURE 3.2   Optimal *f* Is an *Asymptote*

know exactly how many holding periods we are going to play for, and there is consolation in the fact that what we are calling the optimal *f* approaches what would be optimal to maximize EACG as more holding periods elapse.

People tend, mistakenly, to think that the straight line of the "one-shot-expectation," which we saw previously in Figure 3.1, simply remains a straight line, rising upward as the number of plays increases. However, the reality is that the line actually bends as the number of plays increases, as shown in Figure 3.3.

When we make subsequent plays, our world is no longer flat, but curved.

The reason for this is, simply, that what we have to bet or trade with *today* is a function of what happened to our stake *yesterday.*

The graph in Figure 3.3 shows the multiple we made on our stake, on average, after each play.

You can see the peak of this curve at the optimal value of *f* = .25 for this 2:1 coin toss game. Note that this is the peak for playing this game an infinite number of times; the real peak, the value for *f* that maximizes EACG, a function of the number of holding periods, migrates toward the

----

to the optimal *f* point, however, as that is an asymptote. Thus, to trade at the optimal *f* point, in other words, to satisfy the Kelly criterion (to act so as to maximize the expected value of the logarithm of our capital at each play), does not maximize the growth of capital, and will always be suboptimal. To truly be optimal in terms of maximizing the growth of capital requires that we know, in advance, how many plays or holding periods we will participate in. The resultant *f* value will *always* be more aggressive than that which satisfies the Kelly criterion.

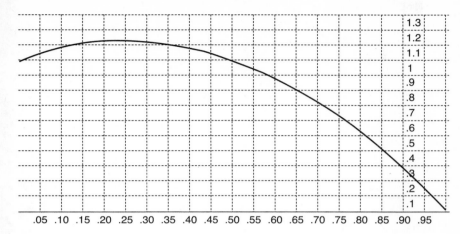

FIGURE 3.3 The Real Line (*f*)

optimal *f* peak from the right of the optimal *f* peak, as the number of plays, the number of holding periods, increases and approaches infinity.

Figure 3.4 shows the graph after 40 plays of our 2:1 coin toss game.

Every trader resides somewhere on this line about the *f* spectrum, because as we saw earlier, we can determine an *f* value based on how many units you have on, for a given level of equity, and a given perceived worst case loss. And these inputs are all givens. Thus, at any point in time, we can take any trader, trading any market system, and assign an *f* value to him, to where he resides on a similar curve.

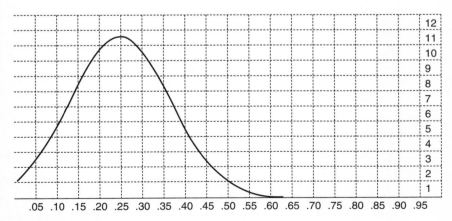

FIGURE 3.4 *f* After 40 Plays

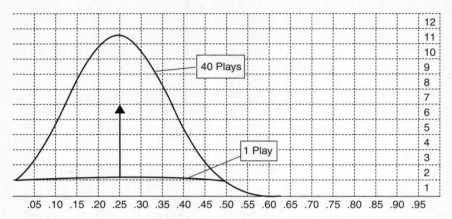

FIGURE 3.5 *f* After 40 Plays (versus 1 Play)

There is always a curve to this function, and it has just one peak. Therefore, where the trader's *f* is with respect to the peak will dictate what kind of gain the trader is looking at, what kind of drawdown he is looking at, and so on. Different locations on this curve have rather dramatic consequences and benefits.

We also know that every point along the curve (every value of *f*) can be converted to an amount by which a market system can be capitalized. Thus, at the peak at *f* = .25 we risk \$1 (worst-case outcome) for every \$4 in our stake. Similarly, a given level of account equity, with a certain number of positions in a certain market system and a certain worst-case outcome, can be converted to an *f* value and located somewhere on the *f* spectrum.

Again, if the worst-case outcome is incorrect, you are still somewhere on the *f* spectrum, and the curve is still identical to the case of the known worst-case outcome's loss, except that it (*f*) is no longer bounded between 0 and 1; rather, it is now bounded between 0 and some other number. The shape of the curve thus stretches or shrinks accordingly; if the curve be bounded between 0 and 2 say, the peak in this instance would thus be at .5. Everything else remains the same. The optimal *f*\$ (the optimal amount to finance each trade by), that is, the optimal number of contracts to have on for a given level of equity, is unchanged.)

The difference in terms of gain, of being at the optimal and any other point, is magnified as time passes, as holding periods increase, as depicted in Figure 3.5.

By bounding *f* between 0 and 1, we can therefore state that when the worst-case outcome manifests, our drawdown is at least *f*%.

Thus, the farther left on the spectrum you go (*f* closer to 0), the lower the minimum drawdown.

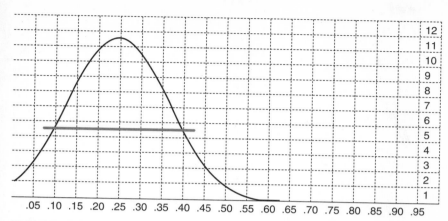

FIGURE 3.6 *f* After 40 Plays: At $f = .1$ and .4, Makes the Same, But Drawdown Changes!

Therefore, *when you dilute* f, *that is, trade at lesser levels of aggressiveness than the optimal* f, *you decrease your drawdowns arithmetically, but you also decrease your returns geometrically.* This difference grows as time goes by. The peak continues to grow and therefore, the price for missing the peak continues to grow.

Paradoxically, the better the system or approach to a given market, the more to the right in the f spectrum (that is, the more toward 1) the peak will be, and hence, the greater will be the minimum drawdown at the optimal f level!

Thus, being to the right makes no more than to the left, but has greater drawdown.

Let us now look at being at an f value of .1 or .4 in our 2:1 coin toss game. This represents taking a 1-unit bet for every 10 units in our stake, and for every 2.5 units in our stake respectively. This is shown in Figure 3.6.

In such a case, our TWR(.1 or .4), the multiple we can expect to make on our stake after 40 plays, is 4.66. This is not even half of what it is at $f = .25$ (where we are making one bet of one unit for every 4 units in our stake), where the TWR(.25) = 10.55, yet we are only 15 percent away from the optimal and only 40 bets have elapsed!

Notice that if we make one bet for every $4 in our stake we will make more than twice as much after 40 bets as you would if you were making one bet for every $2.50 in our stake ($f = .4$)! Clearly it does not pay to overbet. At one bet per every $2.50 in our stake we make the same amount as if we had bet 1/4 that amount, one bet for every $10 in our stake ($f = .1$)!

Also of interest are "points of inflection," $[dTWR(f)/df]$ which are the points at which the curve goes from concave up to concave down (left of

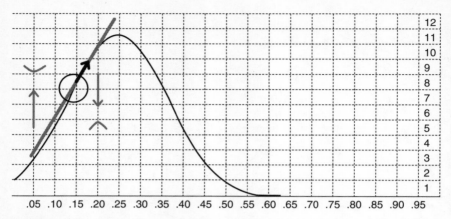

FIGURE 3.7   *f* After 40 Plays. Points of inflection: concave up to concave down. Up has gain growing faster than drawdown (but these too migrate to the optimal point as the number of holding periods grows!).

the peak) and concave down to concave up (right of the peak). Only those left of the peak might be of any use to the investor, however.

When the curve is concave up (left of the peak) we have a growth rate that is increasing ever faster as we increase f (thus, the marginal gain in growth increases with f). As we pass the point of inflection, and go to concave down, this flips and our rate of change in growth, with respect to f, decreases as f increases. See Figure 3.7.

Thus, the point of inflection (left of peak) may be useful to investors as it represents the highest rate of change in growth with respect to changes in f.

Note that the rate of change in the f curve between .15 and .16, for example, is considerably more than between .24 and .25, the difference in terms of raw altitude; the difference in terms of TWR(f) continues to increase as the number of holding periods increases. What may not appear as much of a difference between the exact peak, .25, and a point nearby, .24, actually gets ever greater in terms of difference as the number of holding periods increases.

The problem with the points of inflection (both left and right of the peak) is that they migrate toward the peak as the number of holding periods increases.

As demonstrated in Vince (1995) the problem with what appear to possibly be favorable points in terms of criteria, along the curve, always seem to have the habit of wanting to migrate toward the optimal f peak as the number of holding periods increases [among these, EACG as demonstrated earlier, and the ratio of gain to risk, *TWR(f)/f*].

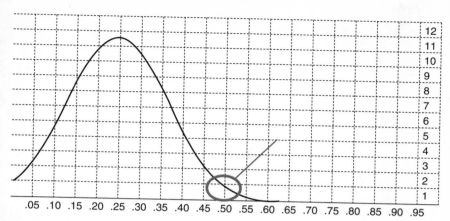

FIGURE 3.8 *f* After 40 Plays. Beyond .5, even in this very favorable game, TWR (Multiple) <1, meaning you are losing money and will eventually go broke if you continue.

Here is another mystery lurking in the dark netherworld, to which investors are oblivious. There is a point, beyond the peak, where the curve—the TWR(f) or GHPR(f)—drops below 1, as shown in Figure 3.8.

In our 2:1 coin toss scenario spectrum example, that point is $f = .5$. Beyond .5 you lose money. This is making one bet for every \$2 in account equity.

Notice! You are not borrowing any money to do this, to assume 1 bet of 1 unit for every 2 units in account equity. It is, in effect, a cash account, no margin is even being used; it is a wildly favorable game, and yet, you go broke with a probability that approaches certainty as you continue to play.

If GHPR(f) < 1 (that is, beyond .5 in this 2:1 coin toss game), at each holding period, each play, the account equity would be expected to be multiplied by a value that is <1. Doing so results in a product that continues toward 0 as the number of holding periods, the number of plays, increases. This is why, even in a game where you win in all but one time out of a million, if you keep doubling your bet (that is, $f = 1.0$) you will go broke with certainty as time increases.

To repeat, nothing is borrowed to do this. It is in a cash account. And every market system has such a point on its f spectrum where ruin is certain as the number of holding periods increases. The only difference between a spectrum of market outcomes and this 2:1 coin toss example, is where the peak is (between 0 and 1) and where this point of certain ruin is (between the peak and 1). The shape of the curve is the same, and the characteristics are the same.

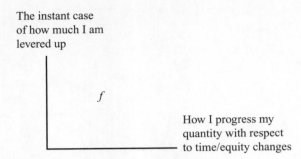

FIGURE 3.9 Leverage Has Two Axes/Two Facets

"Leverage," as I am using the term, is not merely how much one borrows (or, in effect, lends by not only not borrowing, but maintaining a cash position in excess of the value of the asset along with the asset). It is also the schedule upon which that asset position is increased or decreased over time as the account equity fluctuates. "Leverage" refers both to the static snapshot of cash vs. the position itself, and to the schedule of adding to or lightening up on that position. Leverage thus has two facets. As mentioned in the previous chapter, you should think of leverage as the number between 0 and 1 that represents both of these facets, and is articulated by where you are on the f spectrum. See Figure 3.9.

Notice how, just as you are ineluctably at some value for f on the f spectrum, *so too, you ineluctably use "leverage," even in a cash account.* It is vital that you understand that and not be deluded into the false sense of security of trading on a cash basis.

In the past, particularly in the gambling community, the focus has been on the peak itself and not necessarily the nature of the curve. This has led to some bad information and some very poorly derived heuristics regarding the dilution of the optimal point.

One such ad hoc heuristic is the notion of "half Kelly," of which numerous mathematically significant points that migrate might pass through. This is an *arbitrary* (though stationary, with respect to time, that is, holding periods elapsing) point in terms of significance along the curve and is fraught with not understanding the framework. Again, these notions have been perpetuated in much the way that notions about the markets were perpetuated when there were no charts or technical analysis. (For example, "half Kelly" is credited with being able to "give three-quarters of the investment return with much less volatility" than the full optimal f amount. This is patently false, and as the number of plays increases the difference becomes evermore apparent.)

Another example of the ignorance surrounding the nature of the curve is the commonly mentioned notion in the community that "overbetting beyond that suggested by Kelly is counterproductive as the long-run growth rate will fall, dropping to zero when the Kelly bet is approximately doubled."

This is also patently false, and is yet another notion promulgated by ignorance of this curve; this is impossible for a very good system wherein the optimal f value is >.5, and yet every system, however good, has a point where the curve drops below 1.0.

We have discussed the migration from the right to the EACG toward optimal f peak as the number of holding periods increases. We have discussed how, bounding f between 0 and 1, we can expect at least f% drawdown. We have discussed how the difference between being at the optimal point and any other point on the f spectrum grows as the number of holding periods increases. We have looked at how moving to the left on the f curve (between 0 and the optimal f) reduces your drawdowns arithmetically while reducing your gains geometrically. We have seen how, for every profitable point to the left of the peak, there is a point corresponding to the same level of profit on the right of the peak, but with considerably more drawdown. We have seen that there is a point of certain ruin for every market system, even if traded in a cash account (because we have a new, better definition of leverage—that of its having two facets—and we quantify this as the f value, between 0 and 1).

We have taken a peek at how the nature of this curve has been shrouded in ignorance, and we have seen how other mathematically favorable points on this curve, aside from the geometric growth optimal point, tend to migrate toward that geometric growth optimal point (that is, the optimal f) as the number of holding periods (the number of plays) increases.

Whether you like it or not, you are somewhere on this line, this curve on the spectrum of f, when you trade. You have an f value between 0 and 1.

"But I do things in a cash account," you proclaim, "I don't use leverage."

Sure you do. This "leverage" is, in effect, a percentage of the worst-case scenario, and it has nothing to do with margin. If your worst-case scenario is, say, losing $10,000 per "unit" and you have on one unit in a $100,000 account, your f is .1. You are always somewhere on this curve, and the rules detailed here are working upon you whether you acknowledge them or not. I am not trying to sell you on this any more than I am trying to sell you on the notion of gravity!

People spend a lot of time trying to squeeze oil from the rocks of their analysis and systems in an attempt to make them more profitable, when, in fact, profitability is governed exactly as illustrated in Figure 3.4. Every market system, as well as every opportunity under favorable uncertainty,

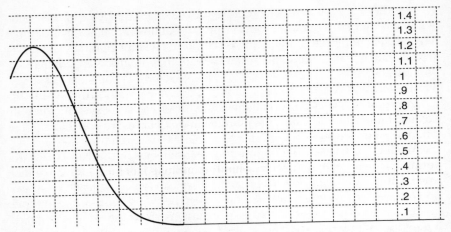

FIGURE 3.10 Very Favorable Blackjack Condition: Optimal $f = .06$ or Risk $1 for Every $16.67 in Stake

has a curve of similar shape where the rules apply, as explained, based on the distribution of outcomes (which can be modeled as scenarios).

Let us consider a card counter in blackjack. There are various flavors of this game, based on rule changes from one type of blackjack to another, and although these rule changes are slight, they can dramatically affect the probabilities involved in the game. There are also differences in the number of decks in the shoe, when the shoe is reshuffled, and there are a plethora of various card-counting strategies available.

Let us assume our card counter, with his technique, is at a particular table, and falls into a very favorable situation where the optimal f was .06. Optimal f changes in a card game just as it does elsewhere. In blackjack, for example, the composition of the remaining cards in the shoe varies from hand to hand. Therefore, the optimal f also changes from hand to hand. In such a situation, the gambler naturally wants to optimize his growth rate. To do so, he must proceed on the immediate play as though that play would be repeated infinitely into the future.

Most blackjack experts will concur this is a very favorable situation, and is depicted in Figure 3.10.

Such a circumstance would have our card-counting gambler ideally bet 1 unit for every 16.67 in his stake. Note that beyond .12, or betting more than one unit for every 8.33 in his stake, the curve drops below 1, and our gambler is doomed to ruin as he continues to play.

Clearly, then, the successful card counter must have a good understanding of how much to bet and when. Absent this, the so-called successful card counter mistakenly attributes his success to his skill, not to simple good luck.

So far, we have discussed the f value assigned to you, unwittingly, when you assume a trade for a given set of possible outcomes on that trade. We can see that we are, therefore, somewhere on some point on the curve, but the payoffs and consequences of being at that point are unknown to us.

(Readers not interested in the mathematical basis can skip directly to Part II here.)

Yet, since we can determine that curve given the scenarios, we are able to determine where the optimal point is on that curve. We seek to find that optimal point (between 0 and 1), that f value that maximizes the Geometric Mean HPR, GHPR(f). To do so, we must amend our technique for determining GHPR(f), to discern what the optimal f is for a given scenario spectrum.

$$GHPR(f) = \prod_{i=1}^{n} HPR(f)_i \qquad (3.01)$$

In determining this, we amend our Holding Period Return, HPR(f):

$$HPR(f)_i = \left(1 + \frac{A_i}{\frac{-W}{f}}\right)^{P_i} \qquad (3.02)$$

So GHPR(f) can also be expressed as:

$$GHPR(f) = \prod_{i=1}^{n} \left(\left(1 + \frac{A_i}{\frac{-W}{f}}\right)^{P_i}\right) \qquad (3.01a)$$

and finally, TWR(f), the multiple on our stake after N periods have elapsed is:

$$TWR(f) = GHPR(f)^n = \left(\prod_{i=1}^{n} \left(\left(1 + \frac{A_i}{\frac{-W}{f}}\right)^{P_i}\right)\right)^n \qquad (3.03)$$

or, if after q scenarios have elapsed:

$$TWR(f) = GHPR(f)^q = \left(\prod_{i=1}^{n} \left(\left(1 + \frac{A_i}{\frac{-W}{f}}\right)^{P_i}\right)\right)^q \qquad (3.03a)$$

where: $n =$ the number of different scenarios
     TWR(f) = the Terminal Wealth Relative
     HPR(f)$_i$ = the Holding Period Return of the ith scenario
          A_i = the outcome of the ith scenario
          P_i = the probability of the ith scenario

W = the worst outcome of all N scenarios

f = the value for f which we are testing

q = however many times we want to "expand" this number of periods out

Finding the f that maximizes the geometric mean HPR (or TWR) from this procedure will give us the f that is optimal for all conditions of a single favorable prospect. In other words, it will give you the same answer as the Kelly formulas with the caveats of two possible outcomes (as when two scenarios comprise the entire spectrum of possible outcomes), as well as superseding the earlier 1990 formulas reiterated in Chapter 1. (In effect, those formulas assumed that each trade had an equal probability of occurrence; thus, each trade's outcome is a scenario with a probability of 1 divided by the total number of trades.)

Yet, these formulas, as complete as they are in terms of discerning an optimal f, can determine it for only a single favorable prospect, a single tradable instrument, and a single scenario spectrum. We must now turn our attention to the multiple component case.

Thus, there is one more step, one more set of equations, to discern optimal f, and that will be covered in Part II. Remember the storyline? We needed a means to determine optimal f, bounded between 0 and 1 (which, like the scenario-planning solution formulas provided here, allows for various possibilities to the various outcomes), which applies to multiple, simultaneously played games (that is, portfolios). Such an equation will, as these scenario-planning solutions to optimal f provided here do, supersede the Kelly formulas (applicable in cases where wins are for the same amount and losses are for the same amount) as a subset of a more general solution. The multiple, simultaneous formulations for optimal f, presented next, solve for all of these, including the single case when the number of components therein equals 1. Thus, even the scenario-planning formulas to derive optimal f as provided here are but a subset of what is really needed.

The ultimate answer, provided next, supersedes all others.

MATHEMATICAL ADDENDUM TO PART I: THE SINGLE COMPONENT CASE

Readers interested in the mathematics behind the optimal f formulations presented may be interested in some of the geometrical relationships and by-products of the formulations. This material has been presented in earlier books I have written on this topic. I find their study both fascinating as well as revealing about certain important aspects of human behavior regarding allocations in conditions of uncertainty.

This Addendum is not necessary to understand the story that is unfolding. Yet, in terms of understanding how the dark netherworld of quantity of leverage space is illuminated, they are important elements. I provide these here as a recap, reference, and brief introduction for those who have not seen it before.

Geometric Average Trade

One interesting aspect to look at in this exercise is what I call the "Geometric Average Trade," or "GAT(f)." This is the amount you would have made on average, per unit, trading at a given value for f:

$$\text{GAT}(f) = f\$ * (\text{GHPR}(f) - 1) \tag{3.04}$$

Of note here is that GAT(f) is always less than or equal to what most traders call their "average trade," which is the same thing as the Mathematical Expectation (given in the Introduction), which is the Arithmetic Average Trade, or what I call "AAT(f)." Thus we can rephrase a trader's "average trade" as follows, so as to put it into the context we are discussing, and derive the same value for his average trade as he does by:

$$\text{Average Trade} = ME = AAT(f) = f\$ * \left(\frac{\sum_{i=1}^{n} (HPR(f)_i)}{n} - 1 \right) \tag{3.05}$$

and

$$\text{GAT}(f) <= \text{AAT}(f) \tag{3.06}$$

always.

Arithmetic Average HPR, AHPR(f) is incorporated in the above equation as:

$$AHPR(f) = \frac{\sum_{i=1}^{n} (HPR(f)_i)}{n} \tag{3.07}$$

Arithmetic Average HPR(f) is simply the sum of the HPR(f)s divided by n, the number of HPR(f)s.

As you can see, these formulas that are given for discerning GHPR(f) lead to some interesting geometric relationships. Those relationships hold for all calculations of GHPR(f) including the Kelly formulas, as well as the more advanced formulas to follow later in this story. In fact, when we get into multiple, simultaneous plays, that is, portfolios of components, the geometrical relationships are so plentiful as to constitute their own domain of study.

One of the more enlightening relationships here is that of the relationship of GHPR(f) and AHPR(f). These two values happen to be related by the Pythagorean Theorem! This very fact reveals to us some important information about the risks we assume. To clearly see this, we must first understand how to estimate the GHPR(f)s given the individual HPR(f)s.

The Estimated Geometric Mean HPR (or How the Dispersion of Outcomes Affects Geometric Growth)

This discussion will use a gambling illustration for the sake of simplicity. Let's consider two approaches. Approach A wins 10 percent of the time and pays 28 to 1. Approach B wins 70 percent of the time and pays 1 to 1. Our Mathematical Expectation per unit bet for A is 1.9 and for B is .4. Therefore, we can say that for every unit bet Approach A will return, on average, 4.75 times as much as Approach B. However, let's examine this under fixed fractional trading. We can find our optimal fs here by dividing the Mathematical Expectations by the win/loss ratios (per the Kelly formulas). This gives us an optimal f of .0678 for A and .4 for B. The geometric means HPR for each approach at their optimal f levels are then:

$$A = 1.044176755$$
$$B = 1.0857629$$

Approach	% Wins	Win:Loss	*ME*	f	GHPR(f)
A	.1	28:1	1.9	.0678	1.0441768
B	.7	1:1	.4	.4	1.0857629

You can see that Approach B, although less than $1/4$ the Mathematical Expectation of A, makes almost twice as much per bet (returning 8.57629 percent of your entire stake per bet on average when reinvesting at the optimal f levels) as does A (returning 4.4176755 percent of your entire stake per bet on average when reinvesting at the optimal f levels).

Now, assuming a 50 percent drawdown on equity will require a 100 percent gain to recoup, then: 1.044177 to the power of X is equal to 2.0 at approximately X equals 16.5, or more than 16 trades to recoup from a 50 percent drawdown for Approach A. Contrast this to Approach B, where

1.0857629 to the power of X is equal to 2.0 at approximately X equals 9, or nine trades for Approach B to recoup from a 50 percent drawdown.

What's going on here? Is this because Approach B has a higher percentage of winning trades? The reason B is outperforming A has to do with the dispersion of outcomes, and its effect on the growth function. Most people have the mistaken impression that the growth function, the TWR, is:

$$TWR(f) = (1 + r)^q \qquad (3.08)$$

where: r = the interest rate per period, for instance, 7 percent = .07
q = the number of periods

Since $1 + r$ is the same thing as an HPR, we can say that most people have the mistaken impression that the growth function,[3] the TWR, is:

$$TWR(f) = HPR(f)^q \qquad (3.09)$$

This function is only true when the return, that is, the HPR(f), is constant, which is not the case in trading.

The real growth function in trading (or in any event where the HPR(f) is not constant) is the multiplicative product of the HPR(f)s. Assume we are trading coffee, and our optimal $f\$$ is one contract for every 21,000 units in equity, and we have two trades, a loss of 210 units and a gain of 210 units, for HPR(f)s of .99 and 1.01 respectively. In this example, our TWR(f) would be:

$$\begin{aligned} TWR(f) &= 1.01 * .99 \\ &= .9999 \end{aligned}$$

An insight can be gained by using the estimated geometric mean (EGM(f)), which very closely approximates the geometric mean:

$$EGM(f) = \sqrt{AHPR(f)^2 - SDHPR(f)^2} \qquad (3.10)$$

---

[3]Many people mistakenly use the arithmetic average HPR in the equation for HPR^T. As is demonstrated here, this will not give the true TWR after T plays. What you must use is the geometric average HPR, rather than the arithmetic in HPR^T. This will give you the true TWR. If the standard deviation in HPRs is 0, then the arithmetic average HPR and the geometric average HPR are equivalent, and it matters not which you use, arithmetic or geometric average HPR, in such a case.

or:

$$EGM(f) = \sqrt{AHPR(f)^2 - VHPR(f)} \qquad (3.10a)$$

where: $EGM(f) =$ the geometric mean HPR(f)
$AHPR(f) =$ the arithmetic mean HPR(f)
$SDHPR(f) =$ the standard deviation in HPR(f)s
$VHPR(f) =$ the variance in HPR(f)s

Now we take EGM(f) to the power of q (where $q = n$, the total number of periods), to estimate the TWR(f). This will very closely approximate the "multiplicative" growth function, the actual TWR(f):

$$TWR(f) = \left(\sqrt{AHPR(f)^2 - SDHPR(f)^2} \right)^q \qquad (3.11)$$

where: $q =$ the number of periods
$AHPR(f) =$ the arithmetic mean HPR(f)
$SDHPR(f) =$ the standard deviation in HPR(f)s

The insight gained is that we can see here, mathematically, the tradeoff between an increase in the arithmetic average trade versus the dispersion in the trades (their standard deviation or their variance): hence the reason that the 70 percent 1:1 approach did better than the 10 percent 28:1 approach.

Our goal should be to maximize the coefficient of this function, to maximize:

$$EGM(f) = \sqrt{AHPR(f)^2 - VHPR(f)} \qquad (3.10a)$$

Expressed literally, "To maximize the square root of the quantity average HPR squared minus the variance in HPRs."

The exponent of the estimated TWR(f), q, will take care of itself. That is to say that increasing q is not a problem, as we can increase the number of markets we are following, trading more short-term types of systems, and so on.

We can rewrite this equation as:

$$AHPR(f)^2 = EGM(f)^2 + SDHPR(f)^2 \qquad (3.10b)$$

This brings us to the point now where we can envision exactly what the relationships are. Notice that this equation is the familiar Pythagorean Theorem—the hypotenuse of a right-angle triangle squared equals the sum of the squares of its sides! But here, the hypotenuse is AHPR(f), and we want to maximize one of the legs, EGM(f).

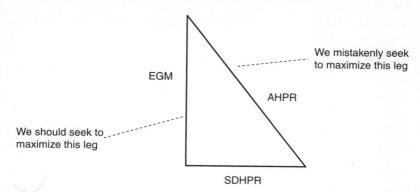

FIGURE 3.11 Triangle Shows We Should Seek to Maximize EGM, Not AHPR

In maximizing EGM(f), any increase in SDHPR(f) will require an increase in AHPR(f) to offset. When SDHPR(f) equals zero, then AHPR(f) equals EGM(f), thus conforming to the misconstrued growth function $TWR = (1 + r)^q$.

So, in terms of their relative effect on EGM(f), we can state that an increase in AHPR(f) is equal to a decrease of the same amount in SDHPR(f), and vice versa. Thus, any amount by which you can reduce the dispersion in trades (in terms of reducing the standard deviation) is equivalent to an increase in the arithmetic average HPR. This is true regardless of whether you are trading at optimal f! Figure 3.11 reveals this.

Additionally, if we are considering a stream of outcomes of only 1 play, the standard deviation is thus 0, and it follows then that the geometric mean equals the arithmetic mean.

If a trader is trading in quantity relative to the size of his stake (and, as we have shown earlier, virtually everyone does), then he wants to maximize EGM(f), not necessarily AHPR(f). In maximizing EGM(f), the trader should realize that the standard deviation, SDHPR(f), affects EGM(f) in directly the same proportion as does AHPR(f), per the Pythagorean Theorem! Thus, when the trader reduces the standard deviation (SDHPR(f)) of his trades, it is equivalent to an equal increase in the arithmetic average HPR (AHPR(f)), and vice versa!

The Fundamental Equation of Trading

We can glean a lot more here than just how trimming the size of our losses, or reducing our dispersion in trades, improves our bottom line. We will return now to the equation for estimating the TWR(f):

$$TWR(f) = \left(\sqrt{AHPR(f)^2 - SDHPR(f)^2} \right)^q \qquad (3.11a)$$

Since $(X^Y)^Z = X^{(Y*Z)}$, we can further simplify the exponents in the equation, thus simplifying this to:

$$TWR(f) = \left(AHPR(f)^2 - SDHPR(f)^2\right)^{q/2} \qquad (3.11b)$$

This last equation is the simplification for the estimated TWR, which we will call the *fundamental equation for trading* because it describes how the different factors, AHPR(f), SDHPR(f), and q, affect our bottom line in trading.

There are a few things that are readily apparent, and the first of these is that if AHPR(f) is less than or equal to 1, then regardless of the other two variables, SDHPR(f) and q, our result can be no greater than 1. If AHPR(f) is less than 1, then as q approaches infinity, AHPR(f) approaches zero. This means that if AHPR(f) is less than or equal to 1 (Mathematical Expectation less than or equal to zero since Mathematical Expectation = AHPR(f) − 1), we do not stand a chance at making profits. In fact, if AHPR(f) is less than 1 it is simply a matter of time until we go broke.

Provided that AHPR(f) is greater than 1, we can see that increasing q increases our total profits. For each increase of one period, the coefficient is further multiplied by its square root.

Each time we can increase q by 1, we increase our TWR(f) by a factor equivalent to the square root of the coefficient (which is the geometric mean). Thus, each time a holding period elapses, each time q is increased by 1, the coefficient is multiplied by the geometric mean.

An important point to note about the fundamental trading equation is that it shows that if you reduce your standard deviation in HPR(f)s to a greater extent than you reduce your arithmetic average HPR(f), you are better off. It stands to reason, therefore, that cutting your losses short, if possible, benefits you. However, the equation demonstrates that at some point you no longer benefit by cutting your losses short. That point is the point where you would be getting stopped out of too many trades with a small loss that later would have turned profitable, thus reducing your AHPR(f) to a greater extent than your SDHPR(f).

Along these same lines, reducing big winning trades can help your program if it reduces your SDHPR(f) more than it reduces your AHPR(f). This can be accomplished, in many cases, by incorporating options into your trading program. Having an option position that goes against your position in the underlying instrument (either by buying long an option or writing an option) can possibly help.

As you can see, the fundamental trading equation can be utilized to dictate many changes in our trading. These changes may be in the way of tightening (or loosening) our stops, setting targets, and so on. These changes are the results of inefficiencies in the way we are carrying out our trading, as well as inefficiencies in our trading program or methodology.

Why Is *f* Optimal?

To see that *f* is optimal in the sense of maximizing wealth:

$$\text{since } GHPR(f) = \left(\prod_{i=1}^{q} HPR(f)_i \right)^{1/q} = \exp \left(\frac{\sum_{i=1}^{q} \ln{(HPR(f)_i)}}{q} \right) \qquad (3.17)$$

If you then act to maximize the geometric mean at every holding period—if the trial is sufficiently long—by applying either the weaker law of large numbers or the central limit theorem to the sum of *independent* variables (that is, the numerator on the right side of this equation), it is almost certain that higher terminal wealth will result than would have by using any other decision rule.

Furthermore, we can also apply Rolle's Theorem to the problem of the proof of *f*s optimality. Recall that we are defining "optimal" here as meaning that which will result in the greatest geometric growth as the number of trials increases. The terminal wealth relative is the measure of average geometric growth, so we want to prove that there is a value for *f* that results in the greatest TWR(*f*).

Rolle's Theorem states that if a *continuous* function crosses a line parallel to the X-axis at two points, *a* and *b*, and the function is continuous throughout the interval *a,b*, then there exists at least one point in the interval where the first derivative equals 0 (that is, at least one relative extreme).

Given that all functions with a positive arithmetic Mathematical Expectation cross the X-axis twice[4] (the X being the *f*-axis) at *f* = 0 and at that point to the right where *f* results in computed HPR(*f*)s where the variance in those HPR(*f*)s exceeds the difference of the arithmetic mean of those HPR(*f*)s minus 1, we have our *a,b* interval on X respectively. Furthermore, the first derivative of the fundamental equation of trading, that is, the estimated TWR(*f*), is continuous for all *f* within the interval, since *f* results in AHPR(*f*)s and variances in those HPR(*f*)s, within the interval, which are differentiable in the function in that interval; thus the function, the estimated TWR(*f*), is continuous within the interval. Per Rolle's Theorem, it must therefore have at least one relative extreme in the interval, and since the interval is positive, that is, above the X-axis, the interval must contain at least one maximum.

---

[4]Actually, at *f* = 0 the TWR = 0, and thus we cannot say that it crosses 0 to the upside here. Instead, we can say that at an *f* value that is an infinitesimally small amount beyond 0, the TWR crosses a line an infinitesimally small amount above 0. Likewise to the right but in reverse, the line, the *f* curve, the TWR, crosses this line which is an infinitesimally small amount above the X-axis as it comes back down to the X-axis.

In fact, there can be only one maximum in the interval given that the change in the geometric mean HPR(f) (a transformation of the TWR(f), given that the geometric mean HPR(f) is the qth root of the TWR(f)) is a direct function of the change in the AHPR(f) and the variance(f), both of which vary in *opposite directions to each other as f varies*, per the Pythagorean Theorem. This guarantees that there can be only one peak. Thus, there must be a peak in the interval, and there can be only one peak. There is an f that is optimal at only one value for f, where the first derivative of the TWR(f) with respect to f equals 0.

In Chapter 1 we saw the 1990 derivation of the TWR(f) as:

$$TWR(f) = \prod_{i=1}^{n}\left(1 + f * \frac{-trade_i}{BiggestLoss}\right) \tag{1.07a}$$

Now we again consider our 2:1 coin toss. There are two trades, two possible scenarios here. If we take the first derivative of this equation with respect to f, we obtain:

$$\frac{dTWR(f)}{df} = ((1 + f * (-trade_1/biggest\,loss)) * (-trade_2/biggest\,loss))$$
$$+ ((-trade_1/biggest\,loss) * (1 + f * (-trade_2/biggest\,loss))) \tag{3.12}$$

If there were more than two trades, the same basic form could be used, but it would quickly grow monstrously large, so we'll only use two trades for the sake of simplicity. Thus, for the sequence $+2, -1$ at $f = .25$:

$$\frac{dTWR(f)}{df} = ((1 + .25 * (-2/-1)) * (-1/-1))$$
$$+ ((-2/-1) * (1 + .25 * (-1/-1)))$$
$$\frac{dTWR(f)}{df} = ((1 + .25 * 2) * -1) + (2 * (1 + .25 * -1))$$
$$\frac{dTWR(f)}{df} = ((1 + .5) * -1) + (2 * (1 - .25))$$
$$\frac{dTWR(f)}{df} = (1.5 * -1) + (2 * .75)$$
$$\frac{dTWR(f)}{df} = -1.5 + 1.5 = 0$$

We now see that the function peaks at .25, where the slope of the tangent is 0, exactly at the optimal f, and no other local extreme can exist because of the restriction caused by the Pythagorean theorem.

Q.E.D. for optimal f existence and as a solitary point in a positive Mathematical Expectation.

Lastly, we will see that optimal f is indifferent to q. We can take the first derivative of the estimated TWR(f) equation with respect to q as:

$$\frac{dTWR(f)}{dq} = \left(AHPR(f)^2 - SDHPR(f)^2\right)^{q/2} * \ln\left(AHPR(f)^2 - SDHPR(f)^2\right)$$

(3.13)

Since $\ln(1) = 0$, then if $AHPR(f)^2 - SDHPR(f)^2 = 1$, that is, $AHPR(f)^2 - 1 = SDHPR(f)^2$ (or variance), the function peaks out and the single optimal maximum TWR(f) is found with respect to f. Notice, though, that both AHPR(f), the arithmetic average HPR(f) and SDHPR(f)—the standard deviation in those HPR(f)s—are not functions of q. Instead they are indifferent to q; thus this equation is indifferent to q at the optimal f. The f that is optimal in the sense of maximizing the estimated TWR(f) will always be the same value regardless of q.

Time Required to Reach a Goal

One other metric should be considered here for interested readers, and that is the time required to reach a particular goal, a particular TWR(f). Simply put, if we have a goal, which is a multiple on our stake that we wish to achieve, then what we have is a target TWR(f). From this, we can determine q, how many holding periods we can expect to elapse to achieve a goal of TWR(f) as:

$$q = \ln(TWR(f))/\ln(GHPR(f))$$ (3.14)

We can alternatively find this as the "Log base GHPR" of the goal by:

$$q = \text{Log}_{GHPR(f)}TWR(f)$$ (3.14a)

These equations are useful in the study of this netherworld of quantity, and we will revisit some of these equations in the sequel. They help illuminate the nature of the curve, as well as the payoffs and consequences of our actions. Clearly, there is far more to geometric mean maximization than merely identifying the peak point in the curve.

PART II

The Multiple Component Case

The Leverage Space Portfolio Model

CHAPTER 4

Multiple, Simultaneous f—"Leverage Space"

T hus far, we have spoken of one game at a time, and of trading a single market, system, portfolio component at a time. Now, we will look at multiple, simultaneous plays, or trading a basket of components, and when we speak of trading multiple components, *we are now speaking about portfolio models.*

We will now see how this notion of optimal f is not merely a method of determining a risk profile, and an optimum point (all of which pertains to us whether we acknowledge it or not), but that this also gives us the building blocks for a portfolio model that is far superior to those that have been employed in one form or another since the middle of the last century.

Since its introduction in 1995, I have referred to this new model as "The Leverage Space Model."

Before we examine the Leverage Space Model, let's first look at the older type of model, which has been in use quite ubiquitously. In doing so, you will see why the Leverage Space Model is superior. The older model is depicted in Figure 4.1.

This graphic demonstrates the traditional approach, the so-called Modern Portfolio Theory approach, also commonly referred to as a "Mean Variance Style Portfolio Model." In this discussion we will simply refer to it as "MPT."

Note in the graphic portfolio that A is preferable to C, as A has less risk for a given level of return. B is preferable to C for a greater return to a given level of risk.

Thus, a "rational" investor, using MPT, wants to be at the upper-leftmost edge of these potential portfolio combinations. This crescent is

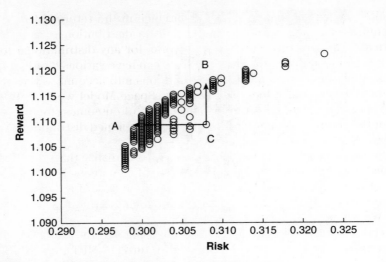

FIGURE 4.1 Modern Portfolio Theory, Reward and Risk

often referred to in the literature as "The Efficient Frontier." A portfolio that lies on the efficient frontier is said to be "efficient" because it maximizes return for a given level of risk, and vice versa.

Return, in MPT ("Reward" on the graphic's vertical axis) is typically characterized by the average return per holding period—essentially what we are referring to herein as AHPR − 1.

Risk, in MPT, the horizontal axis, is defined as variance (standard deviation squared) in holding period returns.

There are four reasons the Leverage Space Model is superior to the MPT-style models:

1. Risk is defined as *drawdown*, not variance in returns.
2. The model is valid for *any* distributional form; *fat tails* are addressed.
3. The Leverage Space Model is about *leverage*, which is not addressed in the traditional models.
4. The fallacy and danger of *correlation* is eliminated.

We have just mentioned risk as being variance (standard deviation squared) in MPT. In the Leverage Space Model, risk is defined as drawdown. How would you rather define risk? Risk is losing your customers, is it not? Ask yourself what it is about your performance that might cause customers to leave. Is the variance in your returns what you really consider your "risk" to be? Is it, perhaps, your drawdowns?

MPT, because it depends on the variance in the returns of its components as a major parameter, assumes the distribution of returns is "Normal." The Leverage Space Model works for any distributional form, and it is assumed that various components can have various distributional forms. MPT cannot take fat-tailed distributions into account, whereas the Leverage Space Model does. The Leverage Space Model works with scenario spectrums as proxies for the distribution of outcomes (that is, proxies for the continuous distributions of which the binned distributions—the scenario spectrum—approximates).

Before we look at the Leverage Space Model, realize that, just as with optimal f in the single component case, as with gravity itself, it *is* and *has been* at work upon you, whether or not you are aware of it. Look at what you're going to see with that in mind, and remember that it is at work on you. We will now articulate it.

The Leverage Space Model, rather than using AHPRs, arithmetic average returns (which are termed "expected" returns in MPT), uses the geometric returns, and not only addresses leverage directly (something MPT completely disregards) but, more importantly, allows us to account for the nature of the curves of each component's f values (along the axis of that component in leverage space), which contain critical information for us as investors. MPT is entirely oblivious to that. The Leverage Space Model is about leverage (in both of its manifestations).

Aside from the "expected" (arithmetic mean) returns and the variance in those returns, MPT requires as an input the correlation coefficients of all of its pairwise components.

The problem with this is that counting on correlation fails you when you need it the most (that is, out on the fat tails of the distribution of outcomes). History shows that most holding periods, most days or most months, are quite incidental. However, there are those few holding periods where big moves *do* occur that can make or break you. It is not at all unlike the game of bridge. You sit, hour after hour, most hands being utterly incidental, until a few unusually distributed hands dictate the ultimate outcome.

MPT is dependent on the correlation of the returns of the various components. The Leverage Space Model is not.

If we look at playing two of our 2:1 coin toss games simultaneously—that is, two scenario spectrums running simultaneously, that is, a portfolio of two components—we would see a correlation coefficient of 0 between the two coin toss games. MPT says you bet (allocate) 50 percent of your stake on each game, but not what the leverage is (thus giving you, in effect, a diagonal line from 0,0 to 1,1 whereupon your location is predicated by how much you opt to lever up). The Leverage Space Model, on the other hand, dictates that you optimally lever to .23,.23. values of f

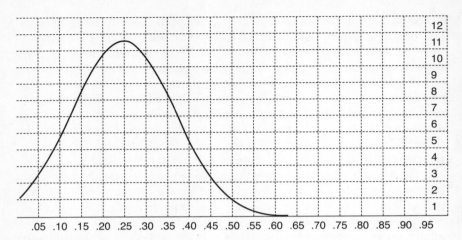

FIGURE 4.2   f for the 2:1 Coin Toss After 40 Plays

for each component (for a total exposure of .46, or 46 percent, of your bankroll).

Now, if the correlation was +1 between the two coin toss games, they would either both win together or both lose together, and it would be the same as playing a single 2:1 coin toss game. If we bet .46 in one game, we are far to the right of the peak. Look at Figure 4.2 to see where .46 puts you on the curve!

If we were playing both games simultaneously, and we thought we had a slightly negative correlation between the two games, when it was positive, we would be way to the right of .46 point!

In Vince (2007) I demonstrate a study I performed using data from a recent 20-year period, looking at the correlations of various and diverse markets. I had equity indexes and various equities, as well as various commodities (oil, gold, and corn).

The purpose of that study was to see what the correlation coefficients became between markets on days where some markets had exceptionally large moves (beyond three standard deviations in price of the previous 200 days).

The results strongly reinforced the fact that correlation fails us on the big move days, which is when we need it most. Without going into the results of the entire study, there are a few samples from the study that demonstrate this characteristic.

For example, if we look at the correlation coefficient, r, of crude oil and gold on all days, we see that $r = .18$. However, on days where crude oil moved three standard deviations or more, r shot up to .61, and on more incidental days, where crude oil moved less than one standard deviation,

r dropped to .09. Clearly, if you were allocating where crude oil and gold were components in a portfolio, and the correlation coefficient of all days was used, .18, you would be terribly overallocated on the big move days when crude oil moves beyond three standard deviations.

If we look at stocks and stock indexes, we see the same principle at work. For example, the correlation coefficient for Ford and Pfizer was .15 for all days. When the S&P 500 index moved in excess of three standard deviations, the correlation coefficient between Ford and Pfizer became .75. If the S&P 500 index moved less than one standard deviation on a given day, the correlation coefficient between Ford and Pfizer dropped to .025.

These correlations, however, were not simply so market related, or between two components, or two components and the index they are a part of. There was a cross-dimensional aspect to this phenomenon.

An example will illustrate this. I looked at corn and Microsoft, for example, on all days that the correlation coefficient over the 20-year period was .02. However, if gold moved by three standard deviations or more, the correlation coefficient between corn and Microsoft shot up to .24, but if gold moved less than one standard deviation, the correlation coefficient between corn and Microsoft dropped to .01.

Using correlation is dangerous as it fails us during those critical periods when we are counting on it the most. Using correlation as an important input to an allocation model will cause us to be badly misled.

In the Leverage Space Model, rather than using correlations as inputs, we simply look at the joint probabilities for each combination of spectrums. In fact, that's the only input we really need!

Coin1	Coin2	Probability
H	H	.25
H	T	.25
T	T	.25
T	H	.25

If I sum up all the probabilities of the first coin being heads, HT and HH, I have .5 as the probability associated with my first coin-as-heads scenario. So, you see, you need only to know scenario outcomes, which are whatever you deem them to be, and then assess the probabilities of the scenario combinations manifesting. All else flows automatically with this model.

What, then, comprises the Leverage Space Model, and how do we construct it?

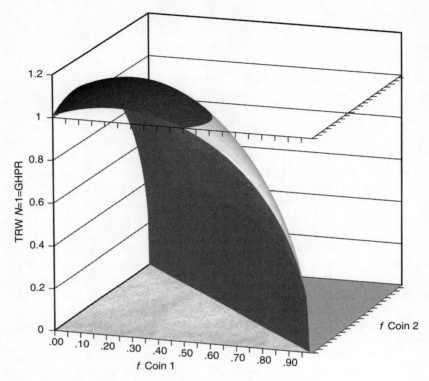

FIGURE 4.3   Coin Toss in 3D, Two Games Simultaneously

Let's go back to our 2:1 coin toss game, where $N = 1$ and we are looking at a curve in the $N+1$-dimensional landscape. The curve is in a 2-dimensional landscape (a plane) for a single game. Figure 4.2 is useful again.

Similarly, if I play two games simultaneously, such as these very same coin toss games simultaneously, $N = 2$ and I am, therefore, looking at a curve in three-dimensional space as shown in Figure 4.3.

This is the basic 2:1 coin toss after one play, but we are playing two games simultaneously. It is the GHPR(f_1, f_2). Note that we have two scenario spectrums ($N = 2$) and four possible outcomes of scenario spectrums ($n = 4$), whereby the probability of each of those four outcomes is .25 in this case.

When we play two games simultaneously, $N = 2$, rather than having a curve such as we have been seeing for the f spectrum, we now have two f spectrums, each with its own axis, making up a surface in 3D space. All of the rules and characteristics we have discussed about the

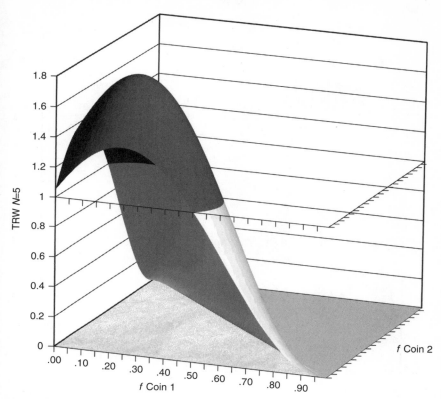

FIGURE 4.4   2:1 Coin Toss in 3D, Five Games Simultaneously

single-component curve in a 2D plane apply in $N+1$-dimensional space, along each of the N-axes.

Thus, in the Leverage Space Model, we have a surface, a "terrain" in $N+1$-dimensional space. (I am showing this with only two components so that we can see it in 3D space.) In Figure 4.4, we see the terrain after five multiple simultaneous plays of our 2:1 coin toss.

Figure 4.5 shows our landscape after 20 multiple, simultaneous plays.

Recall again MPT results in a 50/50 mix of these two components, the leverage left essentially to the discretion of the investor. Yet, as you can plainly see here, the more plays that elapse, the greater the effect on the account by acknowledging and utilizing this portfolio model versus the traditional and misguided MPT ones. If we look at a portfolio of 100 components, we would see a terrain in a 101-dimensional space.

Everything about the single component case pertains here as well—regarding drawdowns, being right of the peak, reducing drawdowns

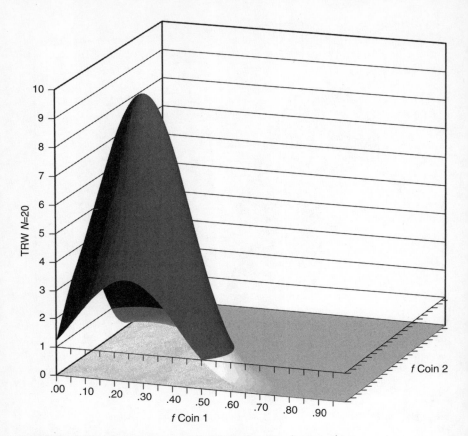

FIGURE 4.5 2:1 Coin Toss in 3D, 20 Games Simultaneously

arithmetically while reducing returns geometrically, and so on—but along two separate axes.

There are some other things that are illuminated by this model that you would not be aware of while using the MPT-style models. For one, notice the area where the surface is <1.0. Note that I can be optimal on one axis, yet so far off on another axis that I can lose money with a probability that approaches certainty if I continue to trade!

Here's something else the older models won't illuminate for you: If I were looking at 101 dimensions, I could be optimal on 99 of the 100 components, yet so far off on one component so as to be <1.0 in altitude, in TWR or GHPR, and hence losing money!

Again, it doesn't matter whether you subscribe to this approach or not—it is at work on you anyway.

You should not be dissuaded by the fallacious notion that the ineluctability of being on this $N+1$-dimensional surface is invalidated by the integer number of units requirement. It does *not* affect what is going on here by one jot.

For example, in the multiple simultaneous 2:1 coin toss case, where our geometric optimal coordinates are .23,.23, we have f of one unit divided by .23, or $1/.23 = 4.347826087$. In other words, we must trade one unit (make one 1-unit bet) per every 4.347826087 units in our stake (on each game, simultaneously).

Now let us further suppose we have a stake of 95 units. We should then place:

$$95/4.347826087 = 21.85$$

Thus, we should bet 21.85 bets of one unit each to be geometrically optimal. However, in the real world, we can bet only in integer units, and since we do not want to be right of the geometrically optimal peak, we should round *down* to the integer 21. That is, we round down to placing 21 bets of one unit each.

The peak still occurs at .23,.23 or one bet for every 4.347826087 units in our stake. However, we are essentially making 21 bets in our stake, or one bet for every $95/21 = 4.523809524$ units in our stake.

From Equation (2.01) we can see:

$$f = |\text{BiggestLoss}|/f\$ \qquad (2.01)$$

Thus, in the instant case, betting one unit for every 4.523809524 units in our stake means the corresponding f coordinate is:

$$f = |-1|/4.523809524 = .221052632$$

Therefore, the optimal point in the $N+1$–dimensional landscape of two multiple, simultaneous 2:1 coin tosses is at .23,.23, while we are—due to the integer unit bet constraint—at .221052632, .221052632. The surface is unchanged, and we are merely shaved "to the left," on all axis. This does not invalidate the fact that you are somewhere on this surface, nor does it change the shape of this surface, or the implications of your location.

Notice that we are looking at the geometric return here. We have already determined that you will trade in quantity relative to the size of your stake, and so it is the geometric return, not the arithmetic, that we must employ in determining the "reward" aspect of our model, as expressed in the graphs as the height of the surface, the TWR(f_1, f_2) for various values of f_1, f_2. This is opposed to the graph of the MPT-style portfolios in which we used, effectively, AHPR-1 as the reward axis.

The Leverage Space Model addresses geometric returns, which are what matter to us, not the fallacious arithmetic returns that the traditional models misguidedly employ, and that erroneously direct our reward focus to the hypotenuse of a right triangle,[1] whereas it is the height of the vertical leg (the geometric return) that is of interest to us.

MPT does not take leverage into account. In sharp contrast, the Leverage Space Model is *all about* leverage. It is based on the notion of optimal *f*, based on the notion of geometric mean maximization, which is entirely about leverage.

In a world of derivative vehicles and notional funding, a portfolio model *must* address leverage head-on. The traditional models ignore the effects of leverage and are ill equipped to model the world in which we work.

In Chapter 3, I noted that "leverage," as I use the term, is not merely how much one borrows (or, in effect, lends by not borrowing and by maintaining a cash position in excess of the value of the asset along with the asset), but is also the schedule upon which that asset position is increased or decreased over time as the account equity fluctuates. The term "leverage" refers to both the static snapshot of cash versus the position itself, and the schedule of adding to or lightening up on that position. Leverage thus has two facets to it. As I said previously, you should think of leverage as the number between 0 and 1 that represents both of these facets, and is articulated by where you are on the *f* spectrum. Again, the traditional models do not address these real-world demands.

(Readers not interested in the mathematical basis can skip directly to Chapter 5 here.)

How, then, do we determine the terrain, the curve, of the $N+1$–dimensional landscape of leverage space? The solution is our ultimate and complete solution not only for determining the curve, the altitude at a coordinate in leverage space, but also for giving us the answer we have long been seeking for discerning the optimal point in that surface—optimal *f* for multiple, simultaneous solutions, bound between 0 and 1 (for each component, or "scenario spectrum") where the probabilities of each potential outcome (scenario) can be different.

The solution gives us the optimal *f* in all cases, even in the simple, single-game case where we always win the same amount and always lose the same amount.

---

[1]See Chapter 3, p. 48, "Mathematical Addendum to Part I: The Single Component Case," regarding "Estimated Geometric Mean HPR (or How the Dispersion of Outcomes Affects Geometric Growth)."

Here, we again determine an HPR for the $N(0 < N < \infty)$ component case:

$$HPR(f_1 \cdots f_N)_k = \left(1 + \left(\sum_{i=1}^{N}\left(f_i * \frac{-PL_{k,i}}{BL_i}\right)\right)\right) \tag{4.01}$$

which again is incorporated into finding the Geometric mean HPR, $GHPR(f_1 \ldots f_N)$, our objective function, the maximum of which constitutes the optimal f set $(f_1 \ldots f_N)$:

$$GHPR(f_1 \cdots f_N) = \prod_{k=1}^{n} HPR(f_1 \ldots f_N)_k^{prob_k} \tag{4.02}$$

Which is therefore expressed as:

$$GHPR(f_1 \cdots f_N) = \prod_{k=1}^{n}\left(\left(1 + \left(\sum_{i=1}^{N}\left(f_i * \frac{-PL_{k,i}}{BL_i}\right)\right)\right)^{prob_k}\right) \tag{4.02a}$$

Finally, we can determine our $TWR(f_1 \ldots f_m)$ after X periods as:

$$TWR(f_1 \cdots f_N) = GHPR(f_1 \cdots f_N)^X \tag{4.03}$$

where: $X =$ however many periods we want to "expand" this out
$N =$ the number of components in the portfolio, the number of scenario spectrums
$n =$ the number of combinations of each scenario, with one scenario from each spectrum; this is the product of the number of scenarios in each spectrum, that is:

$$n = \prod_{i=1}^{N} \#scenarios_i \tag{4.04}$$

For example, if we toss two coins, $N = 2$, and since each scenario has two possible outcomes, heads or tails, $n = 4$. If we were throwing two dice, $N = 2$. Since there are six possible outcomes, $n = 6 * 6 = 36$. Two coins and one die would thus have $N = 3$ and $n = 2 * 2 * 6 = 24$ possible combinations of outcomes.

1. $f_i =$ The value we are using for f of the ith of the $1 \ldots N$ components.
2. $prob_k =$ The probability of the kth combination (of which there are a total of n) of scenarios of the spectrums occurring.

3. $-PL_{k,i}$ = The profit or loss outcome to the scenario of the ith component (scenario spectrum) (from 1 to N) associated with the kth combination of scenarios (from 1 to n).

4. BL_i = The worst outcome scenario of the ith component (scenario spectrum).

Think in terms of a spreadsheet of rows and columns. The following example will make the procedure quite clear in terms of how to implement it. The process of determining the scenarios, their probabilities and payoffs, and even the implementation of the formulas given here to determine their relative optimal f values is far simpler than you may think, as this example will bear out.

Let's suppose I have three separate market systems (thus, "N" in our aforementioned equations is 3), I am trading stocks, and a unit is 100 shares. I am using one year of monthly data here, but you can use periods of any length, whether you want daily, weekly, monthly, yearly, or any other. Typically, longer-term systems will use longer-term data. The allocations I derive, then, will be for monthly allocations to each market system.

First, we need to get into constructing the scenario spectrums for the market systems. We start by taking the net changes in profits and losses of each market system at the end of each period:

	MktSysA	MktSysB	MktSysC
Feb-07	$47.00	$448.00	$381.00
Mar-07	$9.00	$300.00	$799.00
Apr-07	$78.00	−$200.00	$547.00
May-07	$136.00	$321.00	$283.00
Jun-07	−$38.00	−$735.00	$57.00
Jul-07	−$68.00	−$73.00	$317.00
Aug-07	$70.00	$26.00	$140.00
Sep-07	$91.00	$48.00	−$325.00
Oct-07	−$108.00	$122.00	$429.00
Nov-07	−$30.00	−$75.00	$121.00
Dec-07	−$15.00	−$207.00	−$393.00
Jan-08	$2.00	$30.00	$623.00
Feb-08	$22.00	$269.00	$242.00

Notice that all results need to be converted into a common currency. If I use USD as my common currency, I would convert the monthly changes in equity from the currency they are in to USD. Further, I am not basing these conversions on the current basis of that currency to USD, but on the basis of that currency to USD at the end of each particular period.

Next, I determine the range of outcomes for each market system over the entire time window we are considering:

	MktSysA	MktSysB	MktSysC
Min	−$108.00	−$735.00	−$393.00
Max	$136.00	$448.00	$799.00
Range	$244.00	$1,183.00	$1,192.00

I then determine how many bins I want. Suppose I want five bins. I will put the highest and the lowest in their own bins, and I will thus have three bins to cover the inner part of the range. So, I divide the range by 3 in this case:

	MktSysA	MktSysB	MktSysC
Bin Width	$81.33	$394.33	$397.33

From this, I can create the size of the individual bins for each market system that I have, five bins for each, equispaced over the time window that we are considering. (Note that I don't have to have the same number of bins for each market system; I can use a variable number, but in this example, we are using five bins for each market system. Furthermore, they do not necessarily have to be equispaced; I am merely doing that for computational convenience here.)

MktSysA	<	−$108.00
	−$108.00	−$26.67
	−$26.67	$54.67
	$54.67	$136.00
	$136.00	>
MktSysB	<	−$735.00
	−$735.00	−$340.67
	−$340.67	$53.67
	$53.67	$448.00
	$448.00	>
MktSysC	<	−$393.00
	−$393.00	$4.33
	$4.33	$401.67
	$401.67	$799.00
	$799.00	>

We now arrange our data "odometrically" so as to capture every possible combination of occurrence between the scenarios, with one scenario from each spectrum. See Table 4.1. Note that the total number of

TABLE 4.1 Data Arranged Odometrically

MktSysA		MktSysB		MktSysC			
High Range	Low Range	High Range	Low Range	High Range	Low Range	Occurs:	Probability
<	−108	<	−735	<	−393		
<	−108	<	−735	−393	4		
<	−108	<	−735	4	402		
<	−108	<	−735	402	799		
<	−108	<	−735	799	>		
<	−108	−735	−341	<	−393		
<	−108	−735	−341	−393	4		
<	−108	−735	−341	4	402		
<	−108	−735	−341	402	799		
<	−108	−735	−341	799	>		
<	−108	−341	54	<	−393		
<	−108	−341	54	−393	4		
<	−108	−341	54	4	402		
<	−108	−341	54	402	799		
<	−108	−341	54	799	>		
<	−108	54	448	<	−393		
<	−108	54	448	−393	4		
<	−108	54	448	4	402		
<	−108	54	448	402	799	Oct-07	0.076923077
<	−108	54	448	799	>		
<	−108	448	>	<	−393		
<	−108	448	>	−393	4		
<	−108	448	>	4	402		
<	−108	448	>	402	799		
<	−108	448	>	799	>		
−108	−27	<	−735	<	−393		
−108	−27	<	−735	−393	4		
−108	−27	<	−735	4	402	Jun07	0.076923077
−108	−27	<	−735	402	799		
−108	−27	<	−735	799	>		
−108	−27	−735	−341	<	−393		
−108	−27	−735	−341	−393	4		
−108	−27	−735	−341	4	402		
−108	−27	−735	−341	402	799		
−108	−27	−735	−341	799	>		
−108	−27	−341	54	<	−393		
−108	−27	−341	54	−393	4		
−108	−27	−341	54	4	402	Jul-07 7-Nov	0.153846154
−108	−27	−341	54	402	799		
−108	−27	−341	54	799	>		
−108	−27	54	448	<	−393		
−108	−27	54	448	−393	4		

TABLE 4.1 (Continued)

MktSysA		MktSysB		MktSysC			
High Range	Low Range	High Range	Low Range	High Range	Low Range	Occurs:	Probability
−108	−27	54	448	4	402		
−108	−27	54	448	402	799		
−108	−27	54	448	799	>		
−108	−27	448	>	<	−393		
−108	−27	448	>	−393	4		
−108	−27	448	>	4	402		
−108	−27	448	>	402	799		
−108	−27	448	>	799	>		
−27	55	<	−735	<	−393		
−27	55	<	−735	−393	4		
−27	55	<	−735	4	402		
−27	55	<	−735	402	799		
−27	55	<	−735	799	>		
−27	55	−735	−341	<	−393		
−27	55	−735	−341	−393	4		
−27	55	−735	−341	4	402		
−27	55	−735	−341	402	799		
−27	55	−735	−341	799	>		
−27	55	−341	54	<	−393	Dec-07	0.076923077
−27	55	−341	54	−393	4		
−27	55	−341	54	4	402		
−27	55	−341	54	402	799	Jan-08	0.076923077
−27	55	−341	54	799	>		
−27	55	54	448	<	−393		
−27	55	54	448	−393	4		
−27	55	54	448	4	402	Feb-08	0.076923077
−27	55	54	448	402	799		
−27	55	54	448	799	>	Mar-07	0.076923077
−27	55	448	>	<	−393		
−27	55	448	>	−393	4		
−27	55	448	>	4	402	Feb-07	0.076923077
−27	55	448	>	402	799		
−27	55	448	>	799	>		
55	136	<	−735	<	−393		
55	136	<	−735	−393	4		
55	136	<	−735	4	402		
55	136	<	−735	402	799		
55	136	<	−735	799	>		
55	136	−735	−341	<	−393		
55	136	−735	−341	−393	4		
55	136	−735	−341	4	402		
55	136	−735	−341	402	799		

TABLE 4.1 (Continued)

MktSysA		MktSysB		MktSysC			
High Range	Low Range	High Range	Low Range	High Range	Low Range	Occurs:	Probability
55	136	−735	−341	799	>		
55	136	−341	54	<	−393		
55	136	−341	54	−393	4	Sep-07	0.076923077
55	136	−341	54	4	402	Aug-07	0.076923077
55	136	−341	54	402	799	Apr-07	0.076923077
55	136	−341	54	799	>		
55	136	54	448	<	−393		
55	136	54	448	−393	4		
55	136	54	448	4	402		
55	136	54	448	402	799		
55	136	54	448	799	>		
55	136	448	>	<	−393		
55	136	448	>	−393	4		
55	136	448	>	4	402		
55	136	448	>	402	799		
55	136	448	>	799	>		
136	>	<	−735	<	−393		
136	>	<	−735	−393	4		
136	>	<	−735	4	402		
136	>	<	−735	402	799		
136	>	<	−735	799	>		
136	>	−735	−341	<	−393		
136	>	−735	−341	−393	4		
136	>	−735	−341	4	402		
136	>	−735	−341	402	799		
136	>	−735	−341	799	>		
136	>	−341	54	<	−393		
136	>	−341	54	−393	4		
136	>	−341	54	4	402		
136	>	−341	54	402	799		
136	>	−341	54	799	>		
136	>	54	448	<	−393		
136	>	54	448	−393	4		
136	>	54	448	4	402	May-07	0.076923077
136	>	54	448	402	799		
136	>	54	448	799	>		
136	>	448	>	<	−393		
136	>	448	>	−393	4		
136	>	448	>	4	402		
136	>	448	>	402	799		
136	>	448	>	799	>		
							1.0

combinations, the total rows we derive from this exercise, is n in our aforementioned equations. Since we have five scenarios in each spectrum, $n = 5 * 5 * 5 = 125$.

For the Occurs column, I simply take the data from the initial table we created of monthly, common-currency, 1-unit equity changes, taking each row and finding where it corresponds on this sheet. For example, if I take my Feb-08 row of:

	MktSys A	MktSys B	MktSys C
Feb-08	$47.00	$448.00	$381.00

I can see that those three particular outcomes fell into a particular row:

MktSysA		MktSysB		MktSysC		Occurs:
High Range <	Low Range −108	High Range <	Low Range −735	High Range <	Low Range −393	
.	.	.	.	.	.	.
.	.	.	.	.	.	.
.	.	.	.	.	.	.
−27	55	54	448	4	402	Feb-08
.	.	.	.	.	.	.
.	.	.	.	.	.	.
.	.	.	.	.	.	.

Therefore, I recorded it on that row. There is a one-one correspondence between the rows on our first table and this joint-scenarios table. One row on the first will correspond to only one row on this joint-scenarios table.

For the Probability column, I have 13 data points from the original table of monthly, common-currency, 1-unit equity changes. So I take however many data points fall on a row here, divide by 13, and that gives me the joint probability of those scenarios having occurred simultaneously.

Next, we want to specify a single value for each bin, the "A" value for each scenario. There are many ways to do this. One way is to take the mean data point that falls into the bin. In this example, I simply take the average value of the data that falls into a given bin from the original table of monthly, common-currency, 1-unit equity changes.

	High Range	Low Range	Mean Outcome (A)	Row Count/13 (Probabilities) (P)	Data from original table of monthly common-currency, 1-unit equity changes						
MktSysA											
	<	−108	−$108.00	0.076923077	−108						
	−108	−26.66666667	−$45.33	0.230769231	−38	−68	−30				
	−26.66666667	54.66666667	$13.00	0.384615385	47	9	−15	2	22		
	54.66666667	136	$79.67	0.230769231	78	70	91				
	136	>	$136.00	0.076923077	136						
MktSysB											
	<	−735	−$735.00	0.076923077	−735						
	−735	−340.6666667	#DIV/0!	0							
	−340.6666667	53.66666667	−$64.43	0.538461538	−200	−73	26	48	−75	−207	30
	53.66666667	448	$253.00	0.307692308	300	321	122	269			
	448	>	$448.00	0.076923077	448						
MktSysC											
	<	−393	−$393.00	0.076923077	−393						
	−393	4.333333333	−$325.00	0.076923077	−325						
	4.333333333	401.6666667	$220.14	0.538461538	381	283	57	317	140	121	242
	401.6666667	799	$533.00	0.230769231	547	429	623				
	799	>	$799.00	0.076923077	799						

Additionally, we seek to know the probabilities of occurrence at each bin. Since there are 13 data points, we simply see how many data points fall into each bin, and divide by 13. This gives us the "P" value (probability) of each scenario.

Note that it is okay to have joint probability bins with 0 probability (since no empirical data fell into that bin) but it is *not* okay to have scenarios with no outcome value (see the "#DIV/0!" MktSysB for the row −735 to −340.6666667). In such cases, I typically divide the high end plus the low end of the bin by 2 and use that value as the "A" value for that bin (in this case, then, this bin's A value would be −735 + −340.6666667 = −1075.6666667 / 2 = −537.83333334).

Thus, this table can be distilled to the following, which gives us our three scenario spectrums, their outcomes, and associated probabilities:

	Outcome A	Probability P
MktSysA	−$108.00	0.076923077
	−$45.33	0.230769231
	$13.00	0.384615385
	$79.67	0.230769231
	$136.00	0.076923077
MktSysB	−$735.00	0.076923077
	−$537.83	0
	−$64.43	0.538461538
	$253.00	0.307692308
	$448.00	0.076923077
MktSysC	−$393.00	0.076923077
	−$325.00	0.076923077
	$220.14	0.538461538
	$533.00	0.230769231
	$799.00	0.076923077

Alert readers at this point will have calculated the Mathematical Expectation (*ME*) of MktSysA, MktSysB, and MktSysC as 15.08, 21.08, and 247.77 respectively.

Note: In this example, I have used equispaced bins. This is not a requirement; you can use bins of various sizes to try to obtain, say, better resolution around the mode of the bin. Further, as stated, there is no requirement that each scenario spectrum contain the same number of bins or scenarios, even though we are using five scenarios, five bins, for all three spectrums in this example.

It is not uncommon at this point to adjust the outcomes. Often, say, you may wish to make the worst case outcomes for each spectrum a little worse.[2] Thus, you may use something like the following (this is *not* necessary and doing so will not give you what *was* the mathematically optimal f; rather, I am showing it to demonstrate where in the process you may wish to put certain prognostications about the future for use in your work):

	Outcome A	Probability P
MktSysA	−$150.00	0.076923077
	−$45.33	0.230769231
	$13.00	0.384615385
	$79.67	0.230769231
	$136.00	0.076923077
MktSysB	−$1000.00	0.076923077
	−$537.83	0
	−$64.43	0.538461538
	$253.00	0.307692308
	$448.00	0.076923077
MktSysC	−$500.00	0.076923077
	−$325.00	0.076923077
	$220.14	0.538461538
	$533.00	0.230769231
	$799.00	0.076923077

Alert readers will again notice that now the Mathematical Expectations (*MEs*) of MktSysA, MktSysB, and MktSysC have become 11.85, 0.69, and 239.54 respectively.

The final step in this exercise is to amend our joint-scenarios table created earlier to reflect our Outcome ("A") values, rather than the "High Range–Low Range" values we had to use to place our empirical data (the data from the original monthly, common-currency, 1-unit equity changes table) into the appropriate rows.

---

[2]You can amend the joint probabilities table as well, to reflect varying probabilities. For example, I may wish to assume there were 14 data points, rather than 13, and wish to add a single data point to the first row of −150, −1000, −500. Thus, since the total of all the probabilities must equal 1.0, I would amend the other rows that have data in them to reflect this fact (dividing the total number of occurrences at each row by 14). The point is, though using the empirical data, with amendment, will give you the optimal f set, it is but a starting point to the necessary amendments your analysis might call for.

MktSysA	MktSysB	MktSysC	Probability
−$150.00	−$1,000.00	−$500.00	
−$150.00	−$1,000.00	−$325.00	
−$150.00	−$1,000.00	$220.14	
−$150.00	−$1,000.00	$533.00	
−$150.00	−$1,000.00	$799.00	
−$150.00	−$537.83	−$500.00	
−$150.00	−$537.83	−$325.00	
−$150.00	−$537.83	$220.14	
−$150.00	−$537.83	$533.00	
−$150.00	−$537.83	$799.00	
−$150.00	−$64.43	−$500.00	
−$150.00	−$64.43	−$325.00	
−$150.00	−$64.43	$220.14	
−$150.00	−$64.43	$533.00	
−$150.00	−$64.43	$799.00	
−$150.00	$253.00	−$500.00	
−$150.00	$253.00	−$325.00	
−$150.00	$253.00	$220.14	
−$150.00	$253.00	$533.00	0.076923077
−$150.00	$253.00	$799.00	
−$150.00	$448.00	−$500.00	
−$150.00	$448.00	−$325.00	
−$150.00	$448.00	$220.14	
−$150.00	$448.00	$533.00	
−$150.00	$448.00	$799.00	
−$45.33	−$1,000.00	−$500.00	
−$45.33	−$1,000.00	−$325.00	
−$45.33	−$1,000.00	$220.14	0.076923077
−$45.33	−$1,000.00	$533.00	
−$45.33	−$1,000.00	$799.00	
−$45.33	−$537.83	−$500.00	
−$45.33	−$537.83	−$325.00	
−$45.33	−$537.83	$220.14	
−$45.33	−$537.83	$533.00	
−$45.33	−$537.83	$799.00	
−$45.33	−$64.43	−$500.00	
−$45.33	−$64.43	−$325.00	
−$45.33	−$64.43	$220.14	0.153846154
−$45.33	−$64.43	$533.00	

(continues)

MktSysA	MktSysB	MktSysC	Probability
−$45.33	−$64.43	$799.00	
−$45.33	$253.00	−$500.00	
−$45.33	$253.00	−$325.00	
−$45.33	$253.00	$220.14	
−$45.33	$253.00	$533.00	
−$45.33	$253.00	$799.00	
−$45.33	$448.00	−$500.00	
−$45.33	$448.00	−$325.00	
−$45.33	$448.00	$220.14	
−$45.33	$448.00	$533.00	
−$45.33	$448.00	$799.00	
$13.00	−$1,000.00	−$500.00	
$13.00	−$1,000.00	−$325.00	
$13.00	−$1,000.00	$220.14	
$13.00	−$1,000.00	$533.00	
$13.00	−$1,000.00	$799.00	
$13.00	−$537.83	−$500.00	
$13.00	−$537.83	−$325.00	
$13.00	−$537.83	$220.14	
$13.00	−$537.83	$533.00	
$13.00	−$537.83	$799.00	
$13.00	−$64.43	−$500.00	0.076923077
$13.00	−$64.43	−$325.00	
$13.00	−$64.43	$220.14	
$13.00	−$64.43	$533.00	0.076923077
$13.00	−$64.43	$799.00	
$13.00	$253.00	−$500.00	
$13.00	$253.00	−$325.00	
$13.00	$253.00	$220.14	0.076923077
$13.00	$253.00	$533.00	
$13.00	$253.00	$799.00	0.076923077
$13.00	$448.00	−$500.00	
$13.00	$448.00	−$325.00	
$13.00	$448.00	$220.14	0.076923077
$13.00	$448.00	$533.00	
$13.00	$448.00	$799.00	
$79.67	−$1,000.00	−$500.00	
$79.67	−$1,000.00	−$325.00	
$79.67	−$1,000.00	$220.14	
$79.67	−$1,000.00	$533.00	
$79.67	−$1,000.00	$799.00	

MktSysA	MktSysB	MktSysC	Probability
$79.67	−$537.83	−$500.00	
$79.67	−$537.83	−$325.00	
$79.67	−$537.83	$220.14	
$79.67	−$537.83	$533.00	
$79.67	−$537.83	$799.00	
$79.67	−$64.43	−$500.00	
$79.67	−$64.43	−$325.00	0.076923077
$79.67	−$64.43	$220.14	0.076923077
$79.67	−$64.43	$533.00	0.076923077
$79.67	−$64.43	$799.00	
$79.67	$253.00	−$500.00	
$79.67	$253.00	−$325.00	
$79.67	$253.00	$220.14	
$79.67	$253.00	$533.00	
$79.67	$253.00	$799.00	
$79.67	$448.00	−$500.00	
$79.67	$448.00	−$325.00	
$79.67	$448.00	$220.14	
$79.67	$448.00	$533.00	
$79.67	$448.00	$799.00	
$136.00	−$1,000.00	−$500.00	
$136.00	−$1,000.00	−$325.00	
$136.00	−$1,000.00	$220.14	
$136.00	−$1,000.00	$533.00	
$136.00	−$1,000.00	$799.00	
$136.00	−$537.83	−$500.00	
$136.00	−$537.83	−$325.00	
$136.00	−$537.83	$220.14	
$136.00	−$537.83	$533.00	
$136.00	−$537.83	$799.00	
$136.00	−$64.43	−$500.00	
$136.00	−$64.43	−$325.00	
$136.00	−$64.43	$220.14	
$136.00	−$64.43	$533.00	
$136.00	−$64.43	$799.00	
$136.00	$253.00	−$500.00	
$136.00	$253.00	−$325.00	
$136.00	$253.00	$220.14	0.076923077
$136.00	$253.00	$533.00	
$136.00	$253.00	$799.00	

(continues)

MktSysA	MktSysB	MktSysC	Probability
$136.00	$448.00	−$500.00	
$136.00	$448.00	−$325.00	
$136.00	$448.00	$220.14	
$136.00	$448.00	$533.00	
$136.00	$448.00	$799.00	

Furthermore, in our joint-scenarios table, we can disregard any rows where no data occurred. That is, from our joint-scenarios table, we are concerned only with the rows that had at least one empirical data point fall into the Occurs or Probability column. Thus, by paring down this joint-scenarios table, we have the following distillation:

MktSysA	MktSysB	MktSysC	Probability
−$150.00	$253.00	$533.00	0.076923077
−$45.33	−$1,000.00	$220.14	0.076923077
−$45.33	−$64.43	$220.14	0.153846154
$13.00	−$64.43	−$500.00	0.076923077
$13.00	−$64.43	$533.00	0.076923077
$13.00	$253.00	$220.14	0.076923077
$13.00	$253.00	$799.00	0.076923077
$13.00	$448.00	$220.14	0.076923077
$79.67	−$64.43	−$325.00	0.076923077
$79.67	−$64.43	$220.14	0.076923077
$79.67	−$64.43	$533.00	0.076923077
$136.00	$253.00	$220.14	0.076923077

Note that our pared-down joint-scenarios table now has only 12 rows versus the 125 that we started with. We would then, therefore, set $n = 12$ for calculation purposes. At this point, we have gathered together all of the information we need to perform the leverage space calculations.

So we have $N = 3$, and $n = 12$. We want to determine our geometric mean HPR for a given set of f values—of which there are N, or 3—so we seek the maximum GHPR(f_1, f_2, f_3).

We could solve, say, for all values of f_1, f_2, f_3 and plot out the $N+1$–dimensional surface of leverage space (in this case, a four-dimensional surface), or we could apply an optimization algorithm, such as the genetic algorithm, to seek the maximum "altitude," the maximum GHPR(f_1, f_2, f_3). We won't go into the genetic algorithm in this example. Interested readers are referred to Vince (1995 and 2007). Additionally, there are perhaps other optimization algorithms that can be applied here.

Our discussion herein is focused on performing the material that isn't covered in more generalized texts on mathematical optimization.

Notice that to determine the GHPR(f_1, f_2, f_3), we must discern n HPR(f_1, f_2, f_3)s.

$$GHPR(f_1 \cdots f_N) = \prod_{k=1}^{n} HPR(f_1 \ldots f_N)_k^{prob_k} \qquad (4.02)$$

In other words, we go down through each row in the joint probabilities table, calling each row "k," and determine an HPR(k, f_1, f_2, f_3) for each row as follows:

$$HPR(f_1 \cdots f_N)_k = \left(1 + \left(\sum_{i=1}^{N}\left(f_i * \frac{-PL_{k,i}}{BL_i}\right)\right)\right) \qquad (4.01)$$

Notice that inside the $HPR(f_1 \cdots f_N)_k$ formula there is the iteration through each column, each of the N market systems, of which we discern the sum:

$$\sum_{i=1}^{N}\left(f_i * \frac{-PL_{k,i}}{BL_i}\right)$$

Assume we are solving for the f values of .1, .4, and .25 respectively for MktSysA, MktSysB, and MktSysC. We would figure our HPR(.1,.4,.25) at each row in our joint probabilities table, each k, as follows:

$i = 1$	$i = 2$	$i = 3$			MktSysA	MktSysB	MktSysC
				Scenario# (or "k")	$f(.1)*$ $-PL$ $(k, i)/BL_i$ $(f = .1)$	$f(.4)*$ $-PL$ $(k, i)/BL_i$ $(f = .4)$	$f(.25)*$ $-PL$ $(k, i)/BL_i$ $(f = .25)$
MktSysA	MktSysB	MktSysC	Probability				
−$150.00	$253.00	$533.00	0.076923077	1	−0.10	0.10	0.27
−$45.33	−$1,000.00	$220.14	0.076923077	2	−0.03	−0.40	0.11
−$45.33	−$64.43	$220.14	0.153846154	3	−0.03	−0.03	0.11
$13.00	−$64.43	−$500.00	0.076923077	4	0.01	−0.03	−0.25
$13.00	−$64.43	$533.00	0.076923077	5	0.01	−0.03	0.27
$13.00	$253.00	$220.14	0.076923077	6	0.01	0.10	0.11
$13.00	$253.00	$799.00	0.076923077	7	0.01	0.10	0.40
$13.00	$448.00	$220.14	0.076923077	8	0.01	0.18	0.11
$79.67	−$64.43	−$325.00	0.076923077	9	0.05	−0.03	−0.16
$79.67	−$64.43	$220.14	0.076923077	10	0.05	−0.03	0.11
$79.67	−$64.43	$533.00	0.076923077	11	0.05	−0.03	0.27
$136.00	$253.00	$220.14	0.076923077	12	0.09	0.10	0.11

By adding 1 to each of the three rightmost columns, we obtain their HPRs. We can sum these for each row, and obtain a net HPR at that row as 1+ the sum − N(3) as follows:

| i = 1 | i = 2 | i = 3 | | | | | | | | |
MktSysA	MktSysB	MktSysC	Probability	Scenario# (or "k")	MktSysA HPR(.1)	MktSysB HPR(.4)	MktSysC HPR(.25)	Sum	Net HPR (1+Sum-N)	(Net HPR)^P
-$150.00	$253.00	$533.00	0.076923077	1	0.900000	1.101200	1.266500	3.267700	1.267700	1.018414
-$45.33	-$1,000.00	$220.14	0.076923077	2	0.969780	0.600000	1.110070	2.679850	0.679850	0.970753
-$45.33	-$64.43	$220.14	0.153846154	3	0.969780	0.974228	1.110070	3.054078	1.054078	1.008135
$13.00	-$64.43	-$500.00	0.076923077	4	1.008667	0.974228	0.750000	2.732895	0.732895	0.976379
$13.00	-$64.43	$533.00	0.076923077	5	1.008667	0.974228	1.266500	3.249395	1.249395	1.017275
$13.00	$253.00	$220.14	0.076923077	6	1.008667	1.101200	1.110070	3.219937	1.219937	1.015410
$13.00	$253.00	$799.00	0.076923077	7	1.008667	1.101200	1.399500	3.509367	1.509367	1.032175
$13.00	$448.00	$220.14	0.076923077	8	1.008667	1.179200	1.110070	3.297937	1.297937	1.020262
$79.67	-$64.43	-$325.00	0.076923077	9	1.053113	0.974228	0.837500	2.864841	0.864841	0.988892
$79.67	-$64.43	$220.14	0.076923077	10	1.053113	0.974228	1.110070	3.137411	1.137411	1.000953
$79.67	-$64.43	$533.00	0.076923077	11	1.053113	0.974228	1.266500	3.293841	1.293841	1.020014
$136.00	$253.00	$220.14	0.076923077	12	1.090667	1.101200	1.110070	3.301937	1.301937	1.020504
								Geometric Mean HPR=		1.100491443

And multiplying together the HPR^P column, we obtain our GHPR(.1,.4,.25) = 1.00491443.

If we apply a search algorithm (such as the genetic algorithm) to discern the f set that results in the highest GHPR(f_1, f_2, f_3) (or TWR (f_1, f_2, f_3)), we would eventually find the peak at GHPR(.307,0.0,.693) = 1.249. The relative allocations of such an outcome are in the vicinity of:

	f	$f\$$
MktSysA	0.307	$489.17
MktSysB	0	–
MktSysC	0.693	$721.16

For straight scenarios (in which we are using the raw data, not amending the largest loss to be greater losses), the optimal f set is .304, 0.0, .696, which results in a GHPR(.304, 0.0, .696) = 1.339. The relative allocations of such an outcome are in the vicinity of:

	f	$f\$$
MktSysA	0.304	$355.60
MktSysB	0	–
MktSysC	0.696	$564.45

The answer derived from this procedure gives you the optimal f in all cases. It can be used in lieu of the scenario planning formulas presented earlier, in lieu of the 1990 formulas presented earlier as well, and in lieu of the Kelly formulas. It is exact to the extent that the data comprising the scenarios is exact. Bear in mind that the fewer scenarios one uses, the quicker the calculation time, but also the greater amount of information loss that will be suffered.

The procedure is certainly no more difficult than solving for mean variance. Furthermore, there are no parameters whose relevance to the real world is questionable, such as correlation coefficients between pairwise components.

CHAPTER 5

Risk Metrics in Leverage Space and Drawdown

S o far, we have discussed only the return aspect without any real consideration for risk. We have developed a means for determining the optimal f spectrum for multiple, simultaneous components, where each component can have innumerable scenarios, each scenario can have a different probability associated with it, and our answer along each axis (each component's f value) is bounded between 0 and 1. Our story of geometric mean maximization *could* end right there.

We have thus developed a means for determining the return aspect of a potential portfolio model.

However, a portfolio model should have a risk aspect juxtaposed to the return aspect. In the same way that MPT models use the less useful return metric of (arithmetic) average expected return versus the Leverage Space Model using geometric average HPRs for returns, similarly, variance in returns as the risk metric in MPT is supplanted with drawdown as the primary risk metric in the Leverage Space Model.

If we say that along the $N+1$–dimensional surface of leverage space, the given f coordinates there resulted in an expected drawdown that violated a permissible amount, the surface at those coordinates should be replaced with nothing. The surface vanishes at that point—that is, drops to an altitude, a GHPR($f_1 \ldots f_N$) of 0—leaving a location where we cannot reside, thus creating a terrain in the $N+1$–dimensional landscape. A money manager who violates his drawdown constraint faces eventual ruin, and the GHPR, the "altitude" in leverage space, shall reflect that.

Drawdown as a constraint tears the surface, ripping out those uninhabitable locations. If we take, say, a plane that is horizontal to the floor

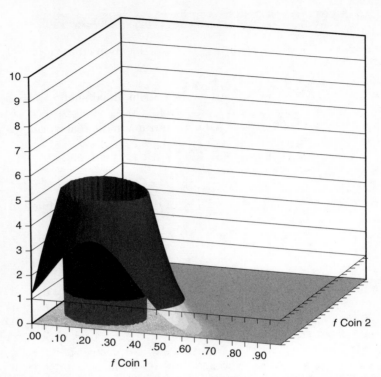

FIGURE 5.1 Coin Toss in 3D, Showing a Drawdown Wherein We Cannot Reside

itself and intersect it with our 2:1 coin toss surface, we get a terrain similar to what is shown in Figure 5.1—a volcano-shaped object, as it were. We cannot reside in the crater because locations there see the terrain drop immediately to 0!

In this example, there are various points on the rim, all with the same TWR(f_1, f_2), since the plane that cuts the surface is parallel to the floor in this example. Thus, a secondary criterion could be employed when there are multiple optimal places in the terrain to select from. For instance, we could invoke a secondary rule that would have us select those coordinates with the lowest sum of all f values; that would put us closer to the 0,0 coordinate, of all the highest points, thus incurring less minimum expected drawdown.

This brings up the point that secondary criteria can also be used along with, or even in lieu of, the drawdown constraint. Let us assume that we create a terrain by removing points on the surface wherein a particular drawdown constraint would be violated. We can further remove terrain if, for example, a particular constraint of a maximum variance is violated, and so on. Similarly, if drawdown is not a concern to us, we might opt to remove surface only from those locations that violated whatever our risk constraint was (for instance, an upper limit on variance, and so on).

In the real world, we rarely see such a simplified shape as shown in Figure 5.1. Planes that are not parallel to any axis, which can themselves be curved and corrugated, usually rip the terrain. In the real world, we tend to see shapes more like those shown in Figure 5.2.

If we take the same shape now, and view it from above, we get a bird's-eye view of the terrain in Figure 5.3.

Look now at how *little* space you have to work with here! Even before the drawdown constraint (if the center of the dark area was filled in) you have very little space to work with. When the drawdown constraint is invoked, the space you have to work with becomes lesser still. Anything not

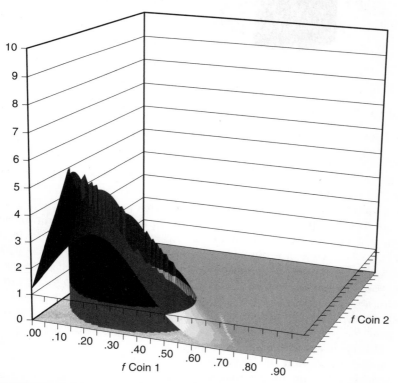

FIGURE 5.2 Real-World, Two-Component Example

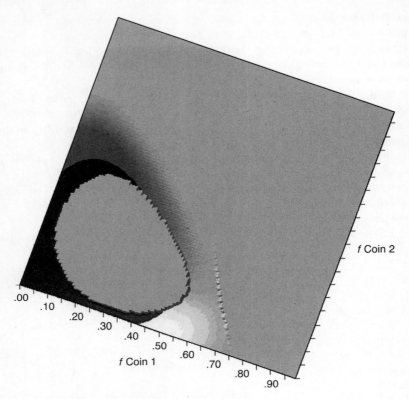

.00
.10
.20
.30
.40
.50
.60
.70
.80
.90

f Coin 1

f Coin 2

FIGURE 5.3 Real-World, Two-Component Example Seen from Above

in the dark area is a location that results in a drawdown that exceeds your drawdown constraint.

Additionally, you can see "from above" that you can be too far off on only one axis, and be in a location that is not acceptable. Also notice that the area with the richest portion of dark area, that is, the areas most likely not to violate a given drawdown constraint, are the areas closer to 0,0. This is why such heuristics in futures trading as to "never risk more than 2 percent on any one trade" (or 1 percent, and so on) developed absent the framework articulated here. They evolved through trial and error, and the framework herein gives explanation as to why such heuristics have evolved. (One might erroneously conclude then that to be tucked deeply toward the 0 . . . 0 point on all axes is simply a good criterion, and accept such heuristics. Recall, however, when we discussed the nature of the curve in Chapter 3, we demonstrated that when we move in a leftward direction of the peak of the optimal f, we decrease our drawdowns arithmetically, but we also decrease our returns geometrically, and this difference grows as time goes by. Furthermore, by tucking in deeply toward 0 . . . 0, we are most likely "to the left of" the points of inflection on the different axes, and thus, if we were to migrate rightward, more toward the peak on the different axes, we would likely see a faster marginal increase in reward than we would risk. Ignorance of the nature of this curve might lead one to believe that returns and drawdowns merely double, say, by going from a 1 percent allocation to a 2 percent allocation. Additionally, this ignorance does not allow one to be as aggressive as he can be in terms of percentage allocation to the respective components while still remaining within his drawdown constraint. These heuristics are a kludgy substitute for what the trader or fund manager has heretofore been ignorant of in the netherworld of leverage space.)

Furthermore, the tighter the drawdown constraint, the less space there is to work with. Obviously, when viewed in this light, ad hoc heuristics such as "half Kelly" and others are hardly germane to what is really going on, whether we acknowledge it or not.

Now let's go back and see what MPT would have us do when viewed in this manner in Figure 5.4.

MPT would put us on that diagonal line between 0,0 and 1,1, representing a 50/50 allocation, leveraged up to the degree of our tastes. Clearly, Nobel prizes notwithstanding, this is not a solution in the real world of drawdowns and leverage. In fact, it will likely lead you into oblivion. It does not illuminate things to the degree we need. The Leverage Space Model, however, provides us with precisely that.

Remember: Ineluctably(!) you use "leverage" even in a cash account, as we demonstrated earlier. Even if you are not borrowing money to carry a position, you are still invoking leverage, you still have an ineluctable coordinate, and those coordinates appear on a map not dissimilar to the one depicted here. The only differences are your drawdown constraints, the number of components you are working with (N), and where the optimal point of those N components is.

The Kelly criterion is simply to bet such as to "maximize the expected value of the logarithm of his capital" (Kelly 1956, p. 925). In other words: to be at the *peak* of the f curve, regardless of its bounds. (*That* is your Kelly criterion—however, remember not to use the so-called Kelly formulas for the solution in finding the curve's peak, as those will work only when there are two scenarios in a single spectrum.) Similarly, Modern Portfolio Theory simply gives a set of points in N dimensions to be at, when in fact, we are in an $N+1$-dimensional manifold (for a single component, it gives a solitary point at 1.0 in the 2-dimensional f-value curve; for two dimensions, a line

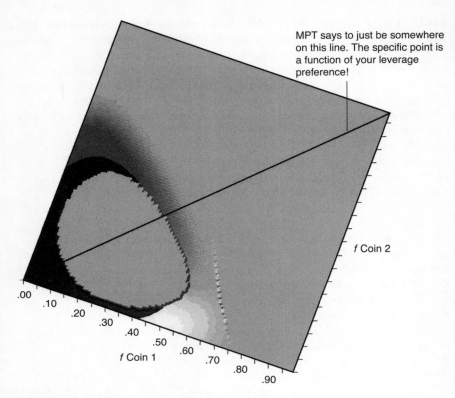

MPT says to just be somewhere on this line. The specific point is a function of your leverage preference!

f Coin 2

.00
.10
.20
.30
.40
.50
.60
.70
.80
.90

f Coin 1

FIGURE 5.4   Real-World, Two-Component Example

in a 3D landscape as depicted in Figure 5.4; in an N component case, a set of points in N dimensions resident in an $N+1$-dimensional landscape). The solutions posited by Modern Portfolio Theory are thus wholly inadequate in the real-world solution space.

(Readers not interested in the mathematical basis can skip directly to Chapter 6 here.)

Let us discuss how to calculate the metric of drawdown.

First, consider the "Classical Gambler's Ruin Problem," according to Feller (Feller 1950, pp. 313–314). Assume a gambler who wins or loses one unit with probability p and $(1 - p)$, respectively. His initial capital is z and he is playing against an opponent whose initial capital is $u - z$, so that the combined capital of the two is u.

The game continues until our gambler, whose initial capital is z, sees it grow to u, or diminish to 0, in which case we say he is *ruined*. It is the probability of this ruin that we are interested in, and this is given by Feller

TABLE 5.1 Results of Risk of Ruin According to Feller, Where *RR* Is the Risk of Ruin: Therefore, 1 − *RR* Is the Probability of Success[1]

Row	p	1 − p	z	u	RR	P (Success)
1	0.5	0.5	9	10	0.1	0.9
2	0.5	0.5	90	100	0.1	0.9
3	0.5	0.5	900	1000	0.1	0.9
4	0.5	0.5	950	1000	0.05	0.95
5	0.5	0.5	8000	10000	0.2	0.8
6	0.45	0.55	9	10	0.210	0.790
7	0.45	0.55	90	100	0.866	0.134
8	0.45	0.55	99	100	0.182	0.818
9	0.4	0.6	90	100	0.983	0.017
10	0.4	0.6	99	100	0.333	0.667
11	0.55	0.45	9	10	0.035	0.965
12	0.55	0.45	90	100	0.000	1.000
13	0.55	0.45	99	100	0.000	1.000
14	0.6	0.4	90	100	0.000	1.000
15	0.6	0.4	99	100	0.000	1.000

as follows:

$$RR = \frac{\left((1-p)/p\right)^u - \left((1-p)/p\right)^z}{\left((1-p)/p\right)^u - 1} \tag{5.01}$$

This equation holds if $(1 - p) \neq p$ (which would cause a division by 0). In those cases where $1 - p$ and p are equal:

$$RR = 1 - \frac{z}{u} \tag{5.01a}$$

Table 5.1 provides results of this formula according to Feller, where *RR* is the risk of ruin. Therefore, $1 - RR$ is the probability of success.

Note in Table 5.1 the difference between row 2, in an even-money game, and the corresponding row 7, where the probabilities turn slightly against the gambler. Note how the risk of ruin, *RR*, shoots upward.

Likewise, consider what happens in row 6, compared to row 7. The probabilities p and $(1 - p)$ have not changed, but the size of the stake and the target *have* changed (z and u—in effect, going from row 7 to row 6 is

---

[1]For the sake of consistency I have altered the variable names in some of Feller's formulas here to be consistent with the variable names I shall be using throughout this chapter.

the same as if we were betting 10 units instead of one unit on each play!). Note also that now the risk of ruin has been cut to less than a quarter of what it was on row 7. Clearly, in a seemingly negative expectation game, one wants to trade in higher amounts and quit sooner. According to Feller,

> *In a game with constant stakes, the gambler therefore minimizes the probability of ruin by selecting the stake as large as consistent with his goal of gaining an amount fixed in advance. The empirical validity of this conclusion has been challenged, usually by people who contend that every "unfair" bet is unreasonable. If this were to be taken seriously, it would mean the end of all insurance business, for the careful driver who insures against liability obviously plays a game that is technically unfair. Actually there exists no theorem in probability to discourage such a driver from taking insurance* (Feller 1950, p. 316).

For our purposes, however, we are dealing with situations considerably more complicated than the simple dual-scenario case of a gambling illustration, and as such we will begin to derive formulas for the more complicated situation. As we leave the classical ruin problem according to Feller, keep in mind that these same principles are at work in investing as well, although the formulations do get considerably more involved.

Let's consider now what we are confronted with mathematically when there are various outcomes involved, and those outcomes are a function of a stake that is multiplicative across outcomes as the sequence of outcomes is progressed through.

Consider again our 2:1 coin toss with $f = .25$:

$$+2, \ -1 \qquad \text{(Stream)}$$
$$1.5, \ .75 \qquad \text{(HPR(.25)s)}$$

There are four possible chronological permutations of these two scenarios as follows, and the terminal wealth relatives (TWRs) that result:

$$1.5 \times 1.5 = 2.25$$
$$1.5 \times .75 = 1.125$$
$$.75 \times 1.5 = 1.125$$
$$.75 \times .75 = .5625$$

Note that the expansion of all possible scenarios into the future is like that put forth when describing Estimated Average Compound Growth in Chapter 3, where we describe optimal f as an asymptote.

Now let's assume we are going to consider that we are ruined if we have only 60 percent ($b = .6$) of our initial stake. Looking at the four outcomes, only one of them ever has your TWR dip to or below the absorbing barrier of .6, that being the fourth sequence of .75 × .75. So, we can state that, in this instance, the risk of ruin of .6 equity left at any time is $\frac{1}{4}$:

$$RR(.6) = \frac{1}{4} = .25$$

Thus, there is a 25 percent chance of drawing down to 60 percent or less on our initial equity in this simple case.

Any time the interim product $<\; = RR(b)$, we consider that ruin has occurred. So in the above example:

$$RR(.8) = \frac{2}{4} = 50 \text{ percent}$$

In other words, at an f value of .25 in our 2:1 coin toss scenario spectrum, half of the possible arrangements of HPR(f)s leave you with 80 percent or less on your initial stake (that is, the last two sequences shown see 80 percent or less at one point or another in the sequential run of scenario outcomes).

Expressed mathematically, we can say that at any i in (5.02) if the interim value for (5.02) $<= 0$, then ruin has occurred:

$$\sum_{i=1}^{q} \left(\left(\prod_{t=0}^{i-1} HPR(f_1 \ldots f_N)_t \right) * HPR(f_1 \ldots f_N)_i - b \right) \tag{5.02}$$

where: $HPR(f_1 \ldots f_N)_0 = 1.0$
$q =$ the number of scenarios in multiplicative sequence (in this case 2, the same as n)[2]
$b =$ that multiple on our stake, as a lower barrier, where we determine ruin to occur ($0 <= b <= 1$)

Again, if at any arbitrary i, we have a value $<=0$, we can conclude that ruin has occurred.

---

[2]For the moment, consider q the same as n. Later in this chapter, they become two distinct variables.

One way of expressing this mathematically would be:

$$\text{int}\left(\frac{\sum_{i=1}^{q}\left(\left(\prod_{t=0}^{i-1} HPR(f_1\ldots f_N)_t\right)*HPR(f_1\ldots f_N)_i - b\right)}{\sum_{i=1}^{q}\left|\left(\left(\prod_{t=0}^{i-1} HPR(f_1\ldots f_N)_t\right)*HPR(f_1\ldots f_N)_i - b\right)\right|}\right) = \beta \qquad (5.03)$$

where: $HPR_0 = 1.0$

q = the number of scenarios in multiplicative sequence

$$\sum_{i=1}^{q}\left|\left(\left(\prod_{t=0}^{i-1} HPR(f_1\ldots f_N)_t\right)*HPR(f_1\ldots f_N)_i - b\right)\right| \neq 0$$

In (5.03) note that β can take only one of two values, either 1 (ruin has not occurred) or 0 (ruin has occurred).

There is the possibility that the denominator in (5.03) equals 0, in which case β should be set to 0.

We digress for purpose of clarity now. Suppose we have a stream of HPR(f)s. Let us suppose we have the five separate HPR(f)s of:

.9
1.05
.7
.85
1.4

Further, let us suppose we determine b, that multiple on our stake, as a lower barrier, where we determine ruin to occur, as .6. Table 5.2 then demonstrates (5.03) and we can thus see that ruin has occurred at $q = 4$.

TABLE 5.2   Demonstrates Equation (5.03)

Q		1	2	3	4	5
HPR(f)		0.9	1.05	0.7	0.85	1.4
TWR(f)	1	0.9	0.945	0.6615	0.562275	0.787185
TWR(f) − .6		0.3	0.345	0.0615	−0.03773	0.187185
TWR(f) − .6 / |TWR(f) − .6|	1	1	1	−1	1

Therefore, we conclude that this stream of HPR(f)s resulted in ruin. (Even though ruin did not occur at the final point, the fact that it occurs at all, at any arbitrary point, is enough to determine that the sequence ruins.)

Using the mathematical sleight-of-hand, taking the integer of the quantity a sum divided by its absolute value (5.03), we derive a value of $\beta = \text{int}(3/5) = \text{int}(.6) = 0$. If the value in column 4 in the last row is 1, then $\beta = 1$.

Note that in (5.03) the HPR(f)s appear to be taken in order; that is, they appear in a single, ordered sequence. Yet, we have four sequences in our example, so we are calculating β for each sequence. Recall that in determining optimal f, sequence does not matter, so we can use any arbitrary sequence of HPR(f)s.

However, in risk of ruin calculations, order *does* matter(!) and we must therefore consider all permutations in the sequence of HPR(f)s. Some permutations at a given set $(b, \text{HPR}(f)_1 \ldots \text{HPR}(f)_n)$ will see $\beta = 0$ while others will see $\beta = 1$. Further, note that for n HPR(f)s, that is, for $\text{HPR}(f)_1 \ldots \text{HPR}(f)_n$, there are n^n permutations.

Therefore, β must be calculated for all permutations of n things taken n at a time. The symbology for this is expressed as:

$$\forall nPn \qquad (5.04)$$

More frequently, this is referred to as "for all permutations of n things taken q at a time," and appears as:

$$\forall nPq \qquad (5.04a)$$

This is the case even though, for the moment in our discussion, $n = q$.

Notice that for n things taken q at a time, the total number of permutations is therefore n^q.

We can take the sum of these β values for all permutations (of n things taken q at a time, and again here, $n = q$ for the moment), and divide by the number of permutations to obtain a real probability of ruin, with *ruin* defined as dropping to b of our starting stake, as $RR(b)$:

$$RR(b, q) = 1 - \frac{\forall nPq \sum_{k=1}^{n^q} \beta_k}{n^q} \qquad (5.05)$$

This is what we are doing in discerning the probability of ruin to a given b, when tossing a single coin two consecutive times. There are two HPR(f)s. Hence there are $2 \times 2 = 4$ permutations, from which we are going to determine a β value for each (using $RR(.6)$). Summing these β values and dividing by the number of permutations, 4, gives us our probability of ruin.

Note the input parameters. We have a value for b in $RR(b)$—that is, the percentage of our starting stake left. Various values for b, of course, will yield various results. Additionally, we are using HPR(f)s, implying that we have an f value here. Different f values will give different HPR(f)s that will give different values for β. Thus, what we are ultimately concerned with here—and the reader is advised at this point to not lose sight of—is that we are essentially looking to hold b constant in our analysis and are concerned with those f values that yield an acceptable $RR(b)$. In other words, we want to find those f values that give us an acceptable probability for a given risk of ruin.

We digress at this point for purposes of clarification. For the moment, let's suspend the notion of each play being a multiple on our stake; we'll suspend thinking of these streams in terms of HPR(f)s and TWR(f)s. Rather, we will simply contemplate the case of being presented with the prospect of three consecutive coin tosses. We can, therefore, say that there are eight separate streams, eight permutations, that the sequence H and T may comprise when being tossed three consecutive times ($\forall_2 P_3$):

H H H
H H T
H T H
H T T (ruin)*
T H H
T H T
T T H (ruin)
T T T (ruin)

Now let us say that if tails occurs in two consecutive tosses, we are ruined. We are trying to determine how many of those eight streams see two consecutive tails. That number, divided by 8 (the number of permutations) is therefore our "Probability of Ruin."

The situation becomes more complex (see H T T (ruin)*) when we add in the concept of multiples. In the previous example, it may be that if the first toss is heads, then two subsequent tosses of tails would not result in ruin, because the first play resulted in enough gain to avert ruin in the two subsequent tosses of tails.

We return now to assigning HPR(f)s to our coin tosses at an optimal f value of .25 and b of .6.

Note what happens as we increase the number of plays. In this case, from two plays (that is, $q = 2$) to three plays ($q = 3$):

$$\forall_2 P_3 =$$
$$1.5 \times 1.5 \times 1.5 = 3.375$$
$$1.5 \times 1.5 \times .75 = 1.6875$$
$$1.5 \times .75 \times 1.5 = 1.6875$$
$$1.5 \times .75 \times .75 = .84375$$
$$.75 \times 1.5 \times 1.5 = 1.6875$$
$$.75 \times 1.5 \times .75 = .84375$$
$$.75 \times .75 \times 1.5 = .84375 \text{ (ruin)}$$
$$.75 \times .75 \times .75 = .421875 \text{ (ruin)}$$

Only the last two sequences saw our stake drop to .6 or less at any time. $RR(.6) = 2/8 = .25$.

Now for four plays:

$$\forall_2 P_4 =$$
$$1.5 \times 1.5 \times 1.5 \times 1.5 = 5.0625$$
$$1.5 \times 1.5 \times 1.5 \times .75 = 2.53125$$
$$1.5 \times 1.5 \times .75 \times 1.5 = 2.53125$$
$$1.5 \times 1.5 \times .75 \times .75 = 1.265625$$
$$1.5 \times .75 \times 1.5 \times 1.5 = 2.53125$$
$$1.5 \times .75 \times 1.5 \times .75 = 2.53125$$
$$1.5 \times .75 \times .75 \times 1.5 = 1.265625$$
$$1.5 \times .75 \times .75 \times .75 = .6328125$$
$$.75 \times 1.5 \times 1.5 \times 1.5 = 2.53125$$
$$.75 \times 1.5 \times 1.5 \times .75 = 1.265625$$
$$.75 \times 1.5 \times .75 \times 1.5 = 1.265625$$
$$.75 \times 1.5 \times .75 \times .75 = .6328125$$
$$.75 \times .75 \times 1.5 \times 1.5 = 1.265625 \text{ (ruin)}$$
$$.75 \times .75 \times 1.5 \times .75 = .6328125 \text{ (ruin)}$$
$$.75 \times .75 \times .75 \times 1.5 = .6328125 \text{ (ruin)}$$
$$.75 \times .75 \times .75 \times .75 = .31640625 \text{ (ruin)}$$

Here, only the last four sequences saw our stake drop to .6 or lower of initial equity at any time. $RR(.6) = 4/16 = .25$.

And now for five plays:

$\forall_2 P_5 =$
1.5 × 1.5 × 1.5 × 1.5 × 1.5 = 7.59375
1.5 × 1.5 × 1.5 × 1.5 × 0.75 = 3.796875
1.5 × 1.5 × 1.5 × 0.75 × 1.5 = 3.796875
1.5 × 1.5 × 1.5 × 0.75 × 0.75 = 1.8984375
1.5 × 1.5 × 0.75 × 1.5 × 1.5 = 3.796875
1.5 × 1.5 × 0.75 × 1.5 × 0.75 = 1.8984375
1.5 × 1.5 × 0.75 × 0.75 × 1.5 = 1.8984375
1.5 × 1.5 × 0.75 × 0.75 × 0.75 = 0.94921875
1.5 × 0.75 × 1.5 × 1.5 × 1.5 = 3.796875
1.5 × 0.75 × 1.5 × 1.5 × 0.75 = 1.8984375
1.5 × 0.75 × 1.5 × 0.75 × 1.5 = 1.8984375
1.5 × 0.75 × 1.5 × 0.75 × 0.75 = 0.94921875
1.5 × 0.75 × 0.75 × 1.5 × 1.5 = 1.8984375
1.5 × 0.75 × 0.75 × 1.5 × 0.75 = 0.94921875
1.5 × 0.75 × 0.75 × 0.75 × 1.5 = 0.94921875
1.5 × 0.75 × 0.75 × 0.75 × 0.75 = 0.474609375 (ruin)
0.75 × 1.5 × 1.5 × 1.5 × 1.5 = 3.796875
0.75 × 1.5 × 1.5 × 1.5 × 0.75 = 1.8984375
0.75 × 1.5 × 1.5 × 0.75 × 1.5 = 1.8984375
0.75 × 1.5 × 1.5 × 0.75 × 0.75 = 0.94921875
0.75 × 1.5 × 0.75 × 1.5 × 1.5 = 1.8984375
0.75 × 1.5 × 0.75 × 1.5 × 0.75 = 0.94921875
0.75 × 1.5 × 0.75 × 0.75 × 1.5 = 0.94921875
0.75 × 1.5 × 0.75 × 0.75 × 0.75 = 0.474609375 (ruin)
0.75 × 0.75 × 1.5 × 1.5 × 1.5 = 1.8984375 (ruin)
0.75 × 0.75 × 1.5 × 1.5 × 0.75 = 0.94921875 (ruin)
0.75 × 0.75 × 1.5 × 0.75 × 1.5 = 0.94921875 (ruin)
0.75 × 0.75 × 1.5 × 0.75 × 0.75 = 0.474609375 (ruin)
0.75 × 0.75 × 0.75 × 1.5 × 1.5 = 0.94921875 (ruin)
0.75 × 0.75 × 0.75 × 1.5 × 0.75 = 0.474609375e (ruin)
0.75 × 0.75 × 0.75 × 0.75 × 1.5 = 0.474609375 (ruin)
0.75 × 0.75 × 0.75 × 0.75 × 0.75 = 0.237304688 (ruin)

Now the probability of ruin has *risen* to 10/32, or .3125. This is very disconcerting, in that the probability of ruin increases the longer you continue to play.

Fortunately, this probability has an asymptote. See what happens with this 2:1 coin toss game, at the optimal f value of .25 per play, in Table 5.3.

From this data, in methods to be detailed later, we can determine that the asymptote, that is, the risk of ruin (defined as 60 percent of our initial

Play #	RR(.6)
2	0.25
3	0.25
4	0.25
5	0.3125
6	0.3125
7	0.367188
8	0.367188
9	0.367188
10	0.389648
11	0.389648
12	0.413818
13	0.413818
14	0.436829
15	0.436829
16	0.436829
17	0.447441
18	0.447441
19	0.459791
20	0.459791
21	0.459791
22	0.466089
23	0.466089
24	0.47383
25	0.47383
26	0.482092

TABLE 5.3 Coin Toss Game, at the Optimal f Value of .25 per Play

equity left in this instance) is .48406 *in the long run sense—that is, if we continue to play indefinitely.*

As shown in Figure 5.5, as q approaches infinity, $RR(b)$ approaches a horizontal asymptote: that is, $RR(b)$ *can* be determined in the long-run sense.

Additionally, it is perfectly acceptable to begin the analysis at $q = 1$, rather than $q = n$. Doing so aids in resolving the line and thus its asymptote.

Remember a very important caveat in this analysis. As demonstrated thus far, it is assumed that there is no statistical dependency in the sequence of scenario outcomes across time. That is, we are looking at the stream of scenario outcomes across time in a pure sample with replacement manner; the past scenario outcome(s) do not influence the current one.

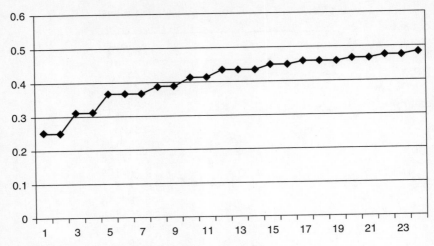

FIGURE 5.5 $RR(.6)$ for 2:1 Coin Toss at $f = .25$

What happens when you have more than a single scenario spectrum? This is easily handled by considering that the HPR(f)s of the different scenario spectrums cover the same time period. That is, we may have our scenarios derived so that they are the scenarios of outcomes for the next month, the next day, and so on.

We therefore consider each combination of scenarios for each scenario spectrum. Thus, if we were looking at two scenario spectrums ($N = 2$) of our 2:1 coin toss, we would then have the following four outcomes (that is, $n = 4$):

$$\text{Game 1} \quad +2 \quad +2 \quad -1 \quad -1$$
$$\text{Game 2} \quad +2 \quad -1 \quad +2 \quad -1$$

The reason we have four outcomes is that we have two scenario spectrums with two scenarios in each. Thus, in this case $n = 4$.

When you have more than one scenario spectrum (that is, $N > 1$):

$$n = \prod_{i=1}^{N} \#scenarios_i \qquad (5.06)$$

where: $N =$ the number of scenario spectrums (components) you are including

In other words, n is the product of all the scenario spectrums we are considering, and in our example here—since there are two scenario spectrums ($N = 2$) each with two scenarios—we have $n = 4$.

The HPR(f)s for these four outcomes, then, are 1 + the sum of HPR(f)s at that period $- N$.

So, if we assume we are going to trade at f values of .25, .25 in our example, we then have the following:

$$
\begin{array}{lrrrr}
\text{Game 1} & +2 & +2 & -1 & -1 \\
\text{Game 2} & +2 & -1 & +2 & -1 \\
\end{array}
$$

Converted to HPR(.25, .25)s:

Game 1	1.5	1.5	.75	.75
Game 2	1.5	.75	1.5	.75
Sum	3	2.25	2.25	1.5
Net HPR (1 + Sum − N)	2	1.25	1.25	.5

Consequently, we have $n = 4$, and the four values are (2, 1.25, 1.25, 5), which we would then use in our analysis.

We digress now. To this point, we have been discussing the probability of ruin, for an aggregate of one or more market systems or scenario spectrums. Risk of ruin $RR(b)$ represents the probability of hitting or penetrating the lower absorbing barrier of $b \times$ initial stake. Thus, this lower absorbing barrier does *not* migrate upward, as equity may increase. If an account therefore increases twofold, this barrier does not move. For example, if $b = .6$ on a million-dollar account, then the lower absorbing barrier is at $600,000. If the account doubles now, to $2 million, then the lower absorbing barrier is *still* at $600,000.

This might be what many want to use in determining our risk metric.

However, far more frequently we want to know the probabilities of touching a lower absorbing barrier from our highest equity point. In other words, we are concerned with risk of drawdown, far more so in most cases than risk of ruin. If our account doubles to $2 million now, rather than being concerned with it going back and touching or penetrating $600,000, we are concerned with it coming down or penetrating double that, or of it coming down to $1.2 million.

This is so much the case that in most instances, for most traders, fund managers, or anyone responsible in a field exposed to risk, it is the *de facto* and organically derived[3] definition of risk itself: "The probability of drawdown," or, more precisely, the probability of a $1 - b$ percentage regression from equity highs, referred to herein now as $RD(b)$.

Again, fortunately, risk of drawdown $[RD(b)]$ is very closely linked to risk of ruin $[RR(b)]$, so much so that we can slide the two in and out of our discussion merely by changing equation (5.03) to reflect risk of drawdown instead of risk of ruin:

$$\text{int}\left(\frac{\sum\limits_{i=1}^{q}\left(\min\left(1.0, \left(\prod\limits_{t=0}^{i-1} HPR(f_1 \ldots f_N)_t \right) \right) * HPR(f_1 \ldots f_N)_i - b \right)}{\sum\limits_{i=1}^{q}\left| \left(\min\left(1.0, \left(\prod\limits_{t=0}^{i-1} HPR(f_1 \ldots f_N)_t \right) \right) * HPR(f_1 \ldots f_N)_i - b \right) \right|} \right) = \beta$$

$$(5.03a)$$

where

$$HPR(f)_0 = 1.0$$

$$\sum\limits_{i=1}^{q}\left| \left(\min\left(1.0, \left(\prod\limits_{t=0}^{i-1} HPR(f_1 \ldots f_N)_t \right) \right) * HPR(f_1 \ldots f_N)_i - b \right) \right| \neq 0$$

Calculating β in subsequent equations by (5.03a) will give you risk of drawdown, as opposed to mere risk of ruin.

The main difference in the mechanics of (5.03a) over (5.03) is that at any time in the running product of HPR(f)s, if the running product is greater than 1.0, then the value 1.0 is replaced for the running product at that point.

Here is some very bare-bones Java code for calculating equation (5.05) for one or more scenario spectrums, for determining either risk of ruin $[RR(b)]$ or risk of drawdown $[RD(b)]$:

```java
import java.awt.*;
import java.io.*;
import java.util.*;
public class MaxTWR4VAR{
    String lines [];
    String msnames [];
    double f [];
    double b;
```

---

[3]All too often, the definition of *risk* in literature pertaining to it has *ignored* the fact that this is exactly what practitioners in the field define risk to be! Rather than the tail wagging the dog here, we opt to accept this real-world definition for risk.

```
    boolean usedrawdowninsteadofruin;
    double plays[][];
    double hprs [][];
    double hpr [];//the composite (arithmetic average per time
//period) of the hprs
    int N; //the number of plays.Capital used to correspond to
//variables in the book
    long NL;// N as a long to avoid many casts
    public MaxTWR4VAR(String[] args){
        try{
            b=Double.parseDouble(args[1]);
        }catch(NumberFormatException e){
            System.out.println("Command Line format: MaxTWR4VAR inputfile
riskofdrawdown(0.0..1.0) calculateRD(true/false)");
            return;
        }
        if(args.length>2){
            usedrawdowninsteadofruin=Boolean.valueOf(args[2]).booleanValue();
        }
        getinputdata(args[0]);
        createHPRs();
        control();
    }

    public static void main(String[] args){
        MaxTWR4VAR maxTWR4VAR = new MaxTWR4VAR(args);
    }

    protected void getinputdata(String fileName){
        String filetext = readInputFile(fileName);
        lines = getArgs(filetext,"\r\n");
        N=lines.length-2;
        NL=(long)N;
        plays=new double[N][];
        for(int i=0;i<lines.length;i++){
            System.out.println("line "+i+" : "+lines[i]);
            if(i==0){
                msnames = getArgs(lines[i],",");
            }else if(i==1){
                f = convertStringArrayToDouble(getArgs(lines[i],","));
            }else{
                plays[i-2]= convertStringArrayToDouble(getArgs(lines[i],","));
            }
        }
        System.out.println("b      : "+b);
        if(usedrawdowninsteadofruin){
            System.out.println("pr of : drawdown");
        }else{
            System.out.println("pr of : ruin");
        }
    }

    protected void  createHPRs(){
        //first find the biggest loss
        double biggestLoss[] = new double [N];
        hprs = new double [plays[0].length][N];
        Arrays.fill(biggestLoss,Double.MAX_VALUE);
```

```
        for(int j=0;j<msnames.length;j++){
            for(int i=0;i<N;i++){
                if(plays[i][j]<biggestLoss[j]){
                    biggestLoss[j]=plays[i][j];
                }
            }
        }
        //fing the hpr for each msnames for each associated f
        for(int j=0;j<msnames.length;j++){
            for(int i=0;i<N;i++){
                hprs[j][i]= 1.0 + f[j] X (-plays[i][j] / biggestLoss[j]);
            }
        }
        //take the arithmetic average of the hprs
        hpr = new double[N];
        for(int i=0;i<N;i++){//go through each play
          for(int j=0;j<msnames.length;j++){ //go through each msnames
              hpr[i] += hprs[j][i];
          }
          hpr[i] = 1.0+hpr[i]-msnames.length
    }
}

protected String readInputFile(String fileName){
    FileInputStream fis = null;
    String str = null;
    try {
        fis = new FileInputStream(fileName);
        int size = fis.available();
        byte[] bytes = new byte [size];
        fis.read(bytes);
        str = new String(bytes);
    } catch (IOException e) {
    } finally {
        try {
            fis.close();
        } catch (IOException e2) {
        }
    }
    return str;
}

protected String[] getArgs(String parameter, String delimiter){
    String args[];
    int nextItem=0;
    StringTokenizer stoke=new StringTokenizer(parameter,delimiter);
    args=new String[stoke.countTokens()];
    while(stoke.hasMoreTokens()){
        args[nextItem]=stoke.nextToken();
        nextItem=(nextItem+1)%args.length;
    }
    return args;
}

protected double [] convertStringArrayToDouble(String [] s){
    double [] d = new double[s.length];
    for(int i = 0; i<s.length; i++){
```

```
                try{
                    d[i]=Double.parseDouble(s[i]);
                }catch(NumberFormatException e){
                    d[i]=0.0;
                }
            }
            return d;
        }


    protected int B(double [] hprset,boolean drawdown){
            double interimHPR=1.0;
            double previnterimHPR=1.0;
            double numerator=0.0;
            double denominator=0.0;
            for(int i=0;i<hprset.length;i++){
                double useinvalue = previnterimHPR;
                if(drawdown && previnterimHPR>1.0)
                    useinvalue = 1.0;

                interimHPR = useinvalue * hprset[i];
                double value = interimHPR - b;
                numerator += value;
                denominator += Math.abs(value);
                previnterimHPR = interimHPR;
            }
            if(denominator==0.0){
                return 0;
            }else{
                double x = (numerator/denominator);
                if(x>=0){
                    return (int)x;
                }else{
                    return 0;
                }
            }
        }


    //n things taken q at a time where q>=n
    //we really cannot use this as we get OutOfMemoryError early on
    //because we try to save the whole array. Instead, use nPq_i()
    protected double[][] nPq(int nopermutations, int q){
            double hprpermutation[][]=new double[nopermutations][q];
            // go through column x column
            for(int column=0;column<q;column++){        // go through
//permutation x permutation
                for(int pn=0;pn<nopermutations;pn++){
                    if(column==0){
                        hprpermutation[pn][column] =  hpr[pn  % N];
                    }else{
                        hprpermutation[pn][column] =
hpr[(pn/(int) (Math.pow((double)N,(double)column))) % N];
                    }
                }
            }
            return hprpermutation;
        }
```

```
//n things taken q at a time where q>=n to return the i'th item
protected double[] nPq_i(int q, long pn){
    double hprpermutation[]=new double[q];
    int x = 0;
    // go through column x column
    for(int column=0;column<q;column++){
        if(column==0){
            x = (int)(pn  % NL);
        }else{
            x = (int)((pn/(long)(Math.pow((double)N,(double)column)))
                 % NL);
        }
        hprpermutation[q-1-column] =  hpr[x];
    }
    return hprpermutation;
}

protected void control(){
    int counter=1;
    while(1==1){
        long passed=0;
        long nopermutations =
                (long) Math.pow((double)hpr.length,(double)counter);
        for(long pn=0;pn<nopermutations;pn++){
            double hprpermutation[]=nPq_i(counter,pn);
            passed+=(long)B(hprpermutation,usedrawdowninsteadofruin);
        }
        double result=1.0-(double)passed/(double)nopermutations;
        System.out.println(counter+" = "+result);
        counter++;
    }
}
}
```

The code is presented "as is," with no warranties whatsoever. Use it as you see fit. It is merely a bare-bones implementation of equation (5.05). I wrote it in as generic a flavor of Java as possible, and intentionally avoided using an object-oriented approach, and intentionally kept it in the lowest-common-denominator syntax across languages, so that you can transport it to other languages more easily. The code can be made *far* more efficient than what is presented here. This is presented merely to give programmers of this concept a starting reference point.

Note that the input file code *must* be formatted as follows: a straight ASCII text file, wherein the first line is the scenario spectrum name, the second line is the f value to be used on that scenario spectrum, and all subsequent lines are the simple stream of individual scenario outcomes. For example:

Coin Toss 1
.25
−1
2

This shows the scenario spectrum "Coin Toss 1" at an f of .25 with two outcomes, one of -1 and the other of $+2$.

To repeat: For situations of multiple scenario spectrums, the first line contains the scenario spectrum names (comma delimited), the second line has the respective f values (comma delimited), and each line after that represents a simultaneous outcome for both scenario spectrums, wherein each combination of scenarios from both scenario spectrums occurs.

```
Coin Toss 1, Coin Toss 2
.25,.25
2,2
2,-1
-1,2
-1,-1
```

So, in this file, the first outcome sees both scenario spectrums gaining two units. The next outcome sees Coin Toss 1 gaining two units while Coin Toss 2 loses one unit (-1). Then Coin Toss 1 loses one unit (-1) and Coin Toss 2 gains two units. For the last outcome, they both lose one unit (-1). (Thus, $n = 4$ in this file. In all data files, therefore, since the first two lines are scenario spectrum name(s) and respective f value(s), n equals the number of lines in the file minus 2.)

To this point, we have not alluded to the probabilities of the scenario outcomes. Rather, as if the scenario outcomes were like a stream of trades, or a stream of coin toss results, we have quietly assumed for simplicity's sake that there has been an equal probability of occurrence with each scenario outcome. In other words, we have been inexplicitly saying to this point that the probability of each scenario (or individual combinations of scenarios from multiple spectrums occurring simultaneously), the probability of the kth outcome among the n^q outcomes, is:

$$p_k = {}^1\!/_{n^q} \tag{5.07}$$

Usually, however, we do not have the luxury or the convenience of all scenarios having the same probability of occurrence.[4]

---

[4]Note, however, that if we *were* talking about scenarios made up of individual coin tosses, or of results of trading a given market system over a given day, or if we used purely empirical data in discerning our scenario spectrums and probabilities, we could use equation (5.07) for the said probabilities. If, for example, we used the last 24 trading months and examined the prices of stock ABC, we could conceivably create a scenario spectrum of 24 bins, each with an outcome of those months, each with a probability given in (5.07).

To address this, we return now to equation (5.05). We will discuss first the case of a single scenario spectrum. In this case, we not only have outcomes for each scenario (which comprise the HPR(f)s used in equation (5.03) or (5.03a) for β), but we also have a probability of its occurrence, p.

$$RX(b, q) = 1 - \frac{\forall nPq \sum_{k=1}^{n^q} (\beta_k * p_k)}{\forall nPq \sum_{k=1}^{n^q} p_k} \qquad (5.05a)$$

where: $\beta =$ the value given in (5.03) or (5.03a)
$\quad\quad\quad p_k =$ the probability of the kth occurrence

For each k, this is the product of the probabilities for that k. That is, you can think of it as the horizontal product of the probabilities from 1 to q for that k. For each k, you calculate a β. Each β_k, as you can see in (5.03) or (5.03a), cycles through from $i = 1$ to q HPR(f)s. Each HPR(f)$_i$ has a probability associated with it ($Prob_{k,i}$). Multiplying these probabilities along as you cycle through from $i = 1$ to q in (5.03) or (5.03a) as you discern β_k will give you p_k in the single scenario case. For example, in a coin toss, where the probabilities are always .5 for each scenario, then whatever the permutation of scenarios in (5.03) or (5.03a), p_k will be $.5 \times .5 = .25$ when $q = 2$ in discerning β_k, for each k, it will equal $.25 \times .25 \times .25 = .015625$ when $q = 3$, *ad infinitum* for the single scenario set case.

$$p_k \prod_{i=1}^{q} Prob_{k,i} \qquad (5.07a)$$

To help dispel confusion, let's return to our simple single coin toss and examine the nomenclature of our variables:

- There is one scenario spectrum: $N = 1$.
- This scenario spectrum has two scenarios: $n = 2$ (per (5.06)).
- We are expanding out in this example to three sequential outcomes, $q = 3$. We traverse this, "horizontally," as $i = 1$ to q (as in (5.03 or 5.03a)).
- Therefore we have $n^q = 2^3 = 8$ sequential outcome possibilities. We traverse this, "vertically," as $k = 1$ to n^q (as in (5.05, 5.05a or 5.05b)).

As we get into multiple scenarios, calculating the individual $Prob_{k,i}$'s gets a little trickier.

There is, then, a probability at a particular i of the manifestations of each individual scenario occurring in N spectrums together (this is a $Prob_{k,i}$). Thus, on a particular i in a (horizontal) multiplicative run from 1 to q, in a particular (vertical) run of k from 1 to n^q, we have a probability $Prob_{k,i}$. Now multiplying these $Prob_{k,i}$'s together in the horizontal run for i from 1 to q will give the p_k for this k.

$$Prob_{1,1} * Prob_{1,2} * \cdots * Prob_{1,q} = p_1$$
$$Prob_{n,1}^q * Prob_{n,2}^q * \cdots * Prob_{n,q}^q = p_n^q$$

n.b., when dependency is present in the stream of outcomes, the p_k values are necessarily affected.

For example, in the simplistic binomial outcome case of a coin toss ($N = 1$), where I have two possible outcomes ($n = 2$), heads and tails, with outcomes $+2$ and -1, respectively, and I look at flipping the coin two times ($q = 2$), I have the following four (n^q) possible outcomes:

				p_k
Outcome 1	$(k = 1)$	H	H	.25
Outcome 2	$(k = 2)$	H	T	.25
Outcome 3	$(k = 3)$	T	H	.25
Outcome 4	$(k = 4)$	T	T	.25

Now assume there is perfect negative correlation involved—that is, winners always beget losers, and vice versa. In this idealized case, we then have the following:

				p_k
Outcome 1	$(k = 1)$	H	H	0
Outcome 2	$(k = 2)$	H	T	.5
Outcome 3	$(k = 3)$	T	H	.5
Outcome 4	$(k = 4)$	T	T	0

Unfortunately, when serial dependency seems to exist, it is never at such an idealized value as 1.0, shown here. Fortunately, however, serial dependency rarely exists, and its appearance of existence in small amounts is usually and typically incidental, and can thus be worked with as being 0. However, if the p_k values are deemed to be more than merely "incidentally serially dependent," then they can be, and in fact, *must be* accounted for as they are used in the equations given in this chapter. The math for doing so is presented as the Addendum to this chapter.

Additionally, the incorporation of rules to address dependency when it seems present, of the type, "Don't trade after two consecutive losers, and so on," could in this analysis be turned into the familiar tails, or T in the following stream:

$$H\ H\ T\ H\ T\ T\ H\ H$$

The dependency rules would transform the stream to

$$H\ H\ T\ H\ T\ T\ H$$

Such a stream could therefore be incorporated into these equations, amended as such, with the same probabilities.

Note the nomenclature in (5.05a), $RX(b, q)$, referring to the fact that this equation can be used for either risk of ruin, $RR(b, q)$, or risk of drawdown, $RD(b, q)$.

Additionally, note that the denominator in this case is simply the sum of the probabilities. Typically, this should equal 1, excepting for floating-point roundoff error. However, this is often not the case when we get into some of the shortcut methods listed later, so (5.05a) will not be rewritten here with a denominator of 1.

The full equation, then, for determining risk of a drawdown $(1 - b)$ at a given q is given as:

$$RD(b, q) = 1 -$$

$$\frac{\forall nPq \sum_{k=1}^{n^q} \left(\text{int} \left(\frac{\sum_{i=1}^{q} \left(\min\left(1.0, \left(\prod_{t=0}^{i-1} HPR(f_1 \ldots f_N)_t\right)\right) * HPR(f_1 \ldots f_N)_i - b\right)}{\sum_{i=1}^{q} \left(\min\left(1.0, \left(\prod_{t=0}^{i-1} HPR(f_1 \ldots f_N)_t\right)\right) * HPR(f_1 \ldots f_N)_i - b\right)} \right)_k * \prod_{i=1}^{q} Prob_{k,i} \right)}{\forall nPq \sum_{k=1}^{n^q} \left(\prod_{i=1}^{q} Prob_{k,i} \right)}$$

$$(5.05\text{b})$$

where:

$$HPR(f_1 \ldots f_N)_0 = 1.0$$

$$\sum_{i=1}^{q} \left| \left(\min\left(1.0, \left(\prod_{t=0}^{i-1} HPR(f_1 \ldots f_N)_t\right)\right) * HPR(f_1 \ldots f_N)_i - b\right) \right| \neq 0$$

Solving (5.05b) will give you the probability of drawdown. Though it looks daunting, the only inputs required to calculate it are a given level of drawdown (expressed as $1 - b$; thus, if I am considering a 20 percent drawdown, I will use $1 - .2 = .8$ as my b value), the f values of the scenario spectrums (from which the $HPR(f_1 \ldots f_N)$s are then derived), and the joint probabilities of the scenarios across the spectrums. In effect, this is all of the information you acquired to construct the altitude of the

Leverage Space Model in the previous chapter (which we determined was no more difficult to gather or construct than an MPT-style model) plus a given drawdown constraint parameter, b. You see, you have already gathered the requisite inputs.

Why is (5.05b) so important? Because you will keep everything in (5.05b) constant, and the only things that will change are the f values of the components in the portfolio, the scenario spectrums from which the HPR(f)s are derived.

Therefore, given (5.05b) one can determine the portfolio that is growth optimal within a given acceptable $RD(b)$! In other words, starting from the standpoint of "I want to have no more than an x percent probability of a drawdown greater than $1 - b$," you can discern the portfolio that is growth optimal.

Essentially then, this new model is:

Maximize TWR($f_1 \ldots f_N$) where $RD(b)$ <= an acceptable probability of hitting b.

This new model, the Leverage Space Model of juxtaposing drawdown to geometric return, is also articulated as:

Find those values for $f_1 \ldots f_N$ which maximize:

$$GHPR(f_1 \ldots f_N) = \prod_{k=1}^{n}\left(\left(1+\left(\sum_{i=1}^{N}\left(f_i * \frac{-PL_{k,i}}{BL_i}\right)\right)\right)^{prob_k}\right)$$

where:

$$1 - \frac{\forall nPq \sum_{k=1}^{n^q}\left(int\left(\frac{\sum_{i=1}^{q}\left(min\left(1.0,\left(\prod_{t=0}^{i-1}HPR(f_1 \ldots f_N)_t\right)\right)*HPR(f_1 \ldots f_N)_i - b\right)}{\sum_{i=1}^{q}\left|\left(min\left(1.0,\left(\prod_{t=0}^{i-1}HPR(f_1 \ldots f_N)_t\right)\right)*HPR(f_1 \ldots f_N)_i - b\right)\right|}\right) * \prod_{i=1}^{q}Prob_{k,i}\right)}{\forall nPq \sum_{k=1}^{n^q}\left(\prod_{i=1}^{q}Prob_{k,i}\right)}$$

is less than or equal to an acceptable probability of hitting b,

where: X = however many periods we want to "expand" this out
        N = the number of components in the portfolio, the number of scenario spectrums
        n = the number of combinations of each scenario, with one scenario from each spectrum; this is the product of the number of scenarios in each spectrum, that is:

$$n = \prod_{i=1}^{N}\#scenarios_i$$

For example, if we are tossing two coins then $N = 2$, and since each scenario has two possible outcomes (heads or tails), $n = 4$. If we were throwing two dice, $N = 2$ and since there are 6 possible outcomes, $n = 6 * 6 = 36$. Two coins and one die would thus have $N = 3$ and $n = 2 * 2 * 6 = 24$ possible combinations of outcomes.

$q = $ the horizon in terms of a number of holding periods

$f_i = $ the value we are using for f of the ith of the $1 \ldots N$ components

$prob_k = $ the probability of the kth combination (of which there are a total of n) of scenarios of the spectrums occurring

$-PL_{k,i} = $ the profit or loss outcome to the scenario of the ith component (scenario spectrum) associated with the kth combination of scenarios

$BL_i = $ the worst-outcome scenario of the ith component (scenario spectrum)

$$HPR(f_1 \ldots f_N)_0 = 1.0$$

$$\sum_{i=1}^{q} \left| \left(\min\left(1.0, \left(\prod_{t=0}^{i-1} HPR(f_1 \ldots f_N)_t \right) \right) * HPR(f_1 \ldots f_N)_i - b \right) \right| \neq 0$$

That is, whenever an allocation is measured in, say, the genetic algorithm for discerning whether it is a new, optimal allocation mix, then it can be measured against (5.05b) given the f values of the candidate mix, the drawdown being considered as $1 - b$, to see whether $RD(b)$, as given by (5.05b), is acceptable (that is, if $RD(b) <= x$).

Additionally, the equation can be looked at in terms of a fund as a scenario spectrum. We can use (5.05), (5.05a), and (5.05b) to determine an allocation to that specific fund in terms of maximum drawdown and maximum risk of ruin probabilities, rather than looking to discern the relative weightings within a portfolio; that is, in the former we are seeking an individual f value that will give us probabilities of drawdowns and ruin that are palatable to us and/or will determine the notional funding amount that accomplishes these tolerable values. In the latter, we are looking for a set of f values to allocate among N components within the portfolio to accomplish the same.

How many q is enough q? How elusive is that asymptote, that risk of drawdown?

In seeking the asymptote to (5.05), (5.05a), (5.05b), we seek that point where each increase in q is met with $RX(b)$ increasing by so slight a margin as to be of no consequence to our analysis. So it would appear that when

$RX(b)$ for a given value of q, $RX(b, q)$ is less than some small amount, a, where we say we are done discerning where the asymptote lies—we can assume that it lies "just above" $RX(b, q)$.

Let's again refer to Figure 5.5. Note that the real-life gradations of $RX(b)$ are not necessarily smooth, but do go upward with spurious stair steps, as it were. So it is not enough to simply say that the asymptote lies "just above" $RX(b, q)$ unless we have gone for a number of iterations, z, before q where $RX(b, q) - RX(b, q - 1) <= a$.

In other words, we can say that we have arrived at the asymptote, and that the asymptote lies "just above" $RX(b, q)$ when, for a given a and z:

$$RX(b, q) - RX(b, q-1) <= a, \quad \text{and} \dots \text{and } RX(b, q) - RX(b, q-z) <= a$$

where:

(5.08)

$$q > z$$

The problem with equation (5.05a) or (5.05b) now is that they increase as q increases, increasing to an asymptote. Note that (5.05a) or (5.05b) will give you the same answer as (5.05) when the probabilities of each kth occurrence are identical.

It is relatively easy to create a chart of the sort shown in Figure 5.5, which is derived from Table 5.3, to attempt to discern an asymptote when $q = 2$ as in our simple 2:1 cointoss situation. However, when we have 26 plays (that is, when we arrive at a value of $q = 26$), then $n^q = 2^{26} = 67,108,864$ permutations.

That's over 67 million β values to compute, and that's just calculating the $RR(b)$ for a single coin-toss scenario spectrum!

When we start getting into multiple scenario spectrums with more than two scenarios each, where n equals the results of (5.06), then clearly, computer power—speed and raw memory requirements—are vital resources in this pursuit.

Suppose I am trying to consider one scenario spectrum ($N = 1$) with 10 scenarios in it ($n = 10$). To make the pass-through merely when $q = n$, I have $10^{10} = 10,000,000,000$ (ten billion) permutations! As we get into multiple scenario spectrums now, the problem explodes on us exponentially.

Most won't have access to the computing resources that this exercise requires for some time. However, we can implement two mathematical shortcuts here to arrive at very accurate conclusions in a mere fraction of the time, in a mere fraction of the computational requirements.

Now, can't I take a random sample of these 10 billion permutations and use that as a proxy for the full 10 billion? The answer is yes, and can be found by statistical measures used for sample size determination for binomially distributed outcomes (note that β is actually a binomial value for whether we have hit a lower absorbing barrier; it is either true or false).

To determine our sample size from binomially distributed data, we will use equation (5.09):

$$\left(\frac{s}{x}\right)^2 *p * (1 - p) \tag{5.09}$$

where: s = the number of sigma (standard deviations) confidence level
            for an error of x
          x = the error level
          p = the probability of the null hypotheses

That last parameter, p, is circularly annoying. If I know p, the probability of the null hypotheses, then why am I sampling to discern, in essence, p?

Note, however, that in (5.09) any deviation in p away from $p = .5$ will give a smaller answer for (5.09). Thus, a smaller sample size would be required for a given s and x, so if we simply set p to .5, we are being conservative, and requiring that (5.09) err on the side of conservatism (that is, as a larger sample size).

To put it more simply, we need only to answer for s and x. So if I want to find the sample size that would give me an error of .001, with a confidence to s standard deviations, solving for (5.09) yields the following:

$$2 \text{ sigma} = \left(\frac{2}{.001}\right)^2 * .5 * (1 - .5) = 1,000,000$$

$$3 \text{ sigma} = \left(\frac{3}{.001}\right)^2 * .5 * (1 - .5) = 2,250,000$$

$$5 \text{ sigma} = \left(\frac{5}{.001}\right)^2 * .5 * (1 - .5) = 6,250,000$$

Now the reader is likely to inquire, "Are these sample sizes independent of the actual population size?" The sample sizes for the given parameters to (5.09) will be the same regardless of whether we are trying to estimate a population of 1,000 or 10,000,000.

"So I need only do this once; I don't need to keep increasing q?"

Not so. Rather, you use equation (5.09) to discern the minimum sample size required at each q. You still need to subsequently increase q, and the answer (as provided by equations (5.05), (5.05a) or (5.05b)) will keep increasing to the asymptote. The reason you must keep increasing q is that at each q, the binomial distribution is different, as demonstrated earlier in this chapter.

One of the key caveats in implementing equation (5.09) is that it is provided for a "random" sample size. However, these minimum, random sample sizes provided for in (5.09) tend to be rather large. Thus, it's important to make sure, since we are generating random numbers by computer, that we are not cycling in our random numbers so soon that it will cause distortion in randomness, and that the random numbers generated be isotropically distributed.

I strongly suggest to the ambitious readers who attempt to program these concepts that they incorporate the most powerful random number generators they can. Over the years this has been something of a moving target, and likely (it is hoped) will continue to be. Currently, I am partial to the Mersenne Twister algorithm (Matsumoto and Nishimura 1998). You can use other random number generators, but your results will be accurate only to the extent of the randomness provided by them.

There are additional real-world implementation issues in terms of adding a floating point number millions of times, considering the floating point roundoff errors, and so on. Ultimately, we are trying to get a "reasonable and real-world workable" resolution of the curves for RR and RD so that we can determine their asymptotes.

This particular shortcut is invoked only if the number of permutations at a given q exceeds n^q. If not, just run all the permutations. For example, where $q = 1$, where we start, there are $10^1 = 10$ permutations. Thus, we just run all 10. At $q = 2$, we have $10^2 = 100$ permutations, and again run all permutations. However, at $10^7 = 10,000,000$, which is greater than the 6,250,000 sample size required, we would begin using the sample size when $q = 7$ in this case.

Let's look at a real-world implementation of what has been discussed thus far. Consider a single scenario spectrum with the following scenarios taken from a real-life trading system, as in Table 5.4.

This is a case of a single scenario spectrum of 10 scenarios. Therefore, on our $n = q$ pass through the data (that is, $q = 10$), we are going to have n^q, or $10^{10} = 10,000,000,000$ (ten billion) permutations, as alluded to earlier.

Now we will attempt to calculate the risk of ruin, with ruin defined as having 60 percent of our initial stake left.

Running these 10 billion calculations outright gives:

$$RR(.6, 10) = .1906955154$$

at an f value of .45.

TABLE 5.4	Single Scenario Spectrum of 10 Scenarios
Outcome	**Probability**
−1889	0.015625
−1430.42	0.046875
−1295	0.015625
−750	0.0625
−450	0.125
0	0.203125
390	0.078125
800	0.328125
1150	0.0625
1830	0.046875

Using (5.09) with $s = 5$, $x = .001$, $p = .5$, we iterate through q obtaining quite nicely, and in a tiny fraction of the time it took to calculate the actual value at $RR(.6, 10)$ just presented (that is, 10 billion iterations for $q = 10$ actually versus 6,250,000! This is .000625 of the time!):

q	$RR(.6)$
1	0.015873
2	0.047367
3	0.07433
4	0.097756
5	0.118505
6	0.136475
7	0.150909
8	0.16485
9	0.178581
10	0.191146
11	0.202753
12	0.209487
13	0.21666
14	0.220812
15	0.244053
16	0.241152
17	0.257894
18	0.269569
19	0.276066
20	1

Note that at $q = 20$ we have $RR(.6) = 1$. This is merely an indication that we have overflowed the value for a long data type in Java.[5] This is still far from the asymptote.

Also note the floating point roundoff error even at $q = 1$. This value should have been 0.015625, not 0.015873.

These calculations were performed by extending the class of the previous Java program earlier in this chapter, and is included herein:

```java
import java.awt.*;
import java.io.*;
import java.util.*;
public class MaxTWR4VARWithProbs extends MaxTWR4VAR{
    double probs[][];
    double probsarray[];
    double probThisB;


    public MaxTWR4VARWithProbs(String[] args){
        super(args);
    }

    public static void main(String[] args){
        MaxTWR4VARWithProbs maxTWR4VARWithProbs =
                    new MaxTWR4VARWithProbs(args);
    }

    protected void getinputdata(String fileName){
        String filetext = readInputFile(fileName);
        lines = getArgs(filetext,"\r\n");
        N=lines.length-2;
        NL=(long)N;
        plays=new double[N][];
        probs=new double[N][lines.length-2];
        for(int i=0;i<lines.length;i++){
            System.out.println("line "+i+" : "+lines[i]);
            if(i==0){
                msnames = getArgs(lines[i],",");
            }else if(i==1){
                f = convertStringArrayToDouble(
                    getArgs(lines[i],","));
            }else{
                plays[i-2]= convertStringArrayToDouble(
                    getArgs(lines[i],","),i-2);
            }
        }
        System.out.println("b     : "+b);
        if(usedrawdowninsteadofruin){
            System.out.println("pr of : drawdown");
        }else{
```

---

[5]Again, all of the code presented here can, even under present-day Java, be made far more efficient and robust than what is shown here. This is merely presented as a starting point for those wishing to pursue these concepts in code.

```
            System.out.println("pr of : ruin");
    }
}

protected double [] convertStringArrayToDouble(
            String [] s,int lineno){
    double [] d = new double[s.length];
    probs[lineno]= new double[s.length];
    for(int i = 0; i<s.length; i++){
        String ss[] = getArgs(s[i],";");
        try{
            d[i]=Double.parseDouble(ss[0]);
            probs[lineno][i]=Double.parseDouble(ss[1]);
        }catch(NumberFormatException e){
            d[i]=0.0;
            probs[lineno][i]=0.0;
        }
    }
    return d;
}

protected int B(double [] hprset,boolean drawdown){
    double interimHPR=1.0;
    double previnterimHPR=1.0;
    double numerator=0.0;
    double denominator=0.0;
    probThisB=1.0;
    for(int i=0;i<hprset.length;i++){
        double useinvalue = previnterimHPR;
        if(drawdown && previnterimHPR>1.0)
            useinvalue = 1.0;
        interimHPR = useinvalue * hprset[i];
        double value = interimHPR - b;
        numerator += value;
        denominator += Math.abs(value);
        previnterimHPR = interimHPR;
        probThisB *= probsarray[i];
    }
    if(denominator==0.0){
        return 0;
    }else{
        double x = (numerator/denominator);
        if(x>=0){
            return (int)x;
        }else{
            return 0;
        }
    }
}

//n things taken q at a time where q>=n to return the i'th item
protected double[] nPq_i(int q, long pn){
    double hprpermutation[]=new double[q];
    probsarray=new double[q];
    int x = 0;
    // go through column x column
    for(int column=0;column<q;column++){                    if(column==0){
```

```
                x = (int)(pn  % NL);
           }else{
                x = (int)((pn/(long)(Math.pow(
                        (double)N,(double)column))) % NL);
           }
           int a = q-1-column;
           hprpermutation[a] = hpr[x];
           //it's zero here because we are only figuring one MS
           probsarray[a] = probs[x][0];            }
       return hprpermutation;
   }


   protected void control(){
       double sigmas = 5.0;
       double errorsize = .001;
       double samplesize = Math.pow(sigmas/errorsize,2.0) X .25;
       long samplesizeL = (long)(samplesize+.5);
       int counter=1;
       RalphVince.Math.MersenneTwisterFast generator = new
RalphVince.Math.MersenneTwisterFast(System.currentTimeMillis());
       java.util.Random random = new java.util.Random();
       while(1==1){
           long permutationcount = 0L;
           double passed=0.0;
           double sumOfProbs=0.0;
           long nopermutations = (long) Math.pow(
                        (double)hpr.length,(double)counter);
           if(nopermutations<(long)samplesize){
               for(long pn=0;pn<nopermutations;pn++){
                   double hprpermutation[]=nPq_i(counter,pn);
                   double theB = (double)B(hprpermutation,
                            usedrawdowninsteadofruin);
                   if(theB>0.0){
                        theB *= probThisB;
                        passed += theB;
                   }
                   sumOfProbs += probThisB;
                   permutationcount++;
               }
           }else{
               do{
                   generator.setSeed(random.nextLong());
                   long pn=(long)(generator.nextDouble()*
                            (double)nopermutations);
                   double hprpermutation[]=nPq_i(counter,pn);
                   double theB = (double)B(hprpermutation,
                            usedrawdowninsteadofruin);
                   if(theB>0.0){
                        theB *= probThisB;
                        passed += theB;
                   }
                   sumOfProbs += probThisB;
                   permutationcount++;

               }while(permutationcount<samplesizeL);
           }
           double result=1.0-passed/sumOfProbs;
```

```
        System.out.println(counter+" = "+result);
        counter++;
    }
  }
}
```

Unlike the previous code provided, this code class works only with one market system ($N=1$), and the format for the input file differs from the first in that in this class, each line from the third line on is a semicolon-delimited value pair of outcome; probability.

Thus, the input file in this real-world example appears as:

```
ten scenario example system
.45
-1889;0.015625
-1430.42;0.046875
-1295;0.015625
-750;0.0625
-450;0.125
0;0.203125
390;0.078125
800;0.328125
1150;0.0625
1830;0.046875
```

The technique of using a random sample gets our first few values for the line of RX to q up and running with very good estimates in short order.

With the second technique, to be presented now, we can extrapolate out that line and hence seek its horizontal asymptote. Fortunately, lines derived from the equations (5.05), (5.05a), and (5.05b) do possess an asymptote and are of this form:

$$RX'(b, q) = \text{asymptote-}variableA * \text{EXP}(-variableB * q) \qquad (5.10)$$

$RX'(b, q)$ will be the surrogate point, the value along the y-axis for a given q along the x-axis in the Cartesian plane.

We can use equation (5.10) as a surrogate for the actual calculations in (5.05),(5.05a), or (5.05b) when q gets too computationally expensive.

To do this, we need only know three values: the asymptote, $variableA$, and $variableB$.

We can find these values by any method of mathematical minimization whereby we minimize the squares of the differences between the observed values and the values given by (5.10). Those values with the minimum sum of the differences squared are those values that best fit this line, this proxy of actual $RX(b, q)$ values when q is too computationally expensive.

The process is relatively simple. We take those values we were able to calculate for $RX(b, q)$. For each of these values, we compare corresponding points derived from (5.10), and square the differences between the two. We then sum the squares.

Thus, we have a sum of the squared differences of our points to (5.10) for a given (asymptote, *variableA*, *variableB*), proceeding with a mathematical minimization routine (Powell's, Downhill Simplex, even the genetic algorithm, though this will be far from the most efficient means). For a list and detailed explanation of these methods, see Press et al. (1986). We arrive at the set of variable values that minimizes the sum of the differences squared between the observed points and their corresponding points as given by (5.10).

Returning, for example, to our 2:1 coin toss, we calculated by equation (5.05) those $RR(.6)$ values, and these were given in Table 5.3. Using Microsoft Excel's Solver function, we can calculate the parameters in (5.10) that yield the best fit:

asymptote	0.48406
variableA	0.37418
variableB	0.137892

The values given by (5.10) are shown in Table 5.5.

This fitted line, equation (5.10), is now shown superimposed as the solid line over Figure 5.5 in Figure 5.6.

Now that we have our three parameters, I can determine for, say, a q of 300, by plugging these values into (5.09), that my risk of ruin ($RR(.6)$) is .484059843.

At a q of 4,000, I arrive at nearly the same number. Obviously, the horizontal asymptote is very much in this vicinity.

The asymptote of such a line is determined, as pointed out earlier in (5.08), since the line given by (5.10) is a smooth one.

Let's go back to our real-world example now, the single scenario set of 10 scenarios. Fitting to our earlier case of a single scenario set with 10 scenarios, whereby we were able to calculate the $RR(.6)$ values for $q = 1 \ldots 19$, by taking 6,250,000 samples for each q (beyond $q = 6$), and using these 10 data points ($q = 1 \ldots 19$) as input to find those values of the parameters in (5.10) that minimize the sum of the squares of the differences between the answers given by those parameters in (5.10) and the actual values we got (by estimating the actual values using (5.09)), gives us the corresponding best-fit parameters for (5.10) as follows:

asymptote=	0.397758
exponent=	0.057114
coefficient	0.371217

TABLE 5.5 Values Given by (5.10)

Play#	Observed (5.05)	Calculated (5.10)
2	0.25	0.200066
3	0.25	0.236646
4	0.25	0.268515
5	0.3125	0.296278
6	0.3125	0.320466
7	0.367188	0.341538
8	0.367188	0.359896
9	0.367188	0.375889
10	0.389648	0.389822
11	0.389648	0.40196
12	0.413818	0.412535
13	0.413818	0.421748
14	0.436829	0.429774
15	0.436829	0.436767
16	0.436829	0.442858
17	0.447441	0.448165
18	0.447441	0.452789
19	0.459791	0.456817
20	0.459791	0.460326
21	0.459791	0.463383
22	0.466089	0.466046
23	0.466089	0.468367
24	0.47383	0.470388
25	0.47383	0.472149
26	0.482092	0.473683

The data points and corresponding function (5.10) then appear graphically as shown in Figure 5.7.

Additionally, if we extend this out to see the asymptote in the function, we can compress the graphic as shown in Figure 5.8.

Using these two shortcuts allows us to accurately estimate what the function for $RX()$ is, and discern where the asymptote is, as well as how many q out it is (since q can be thought of as time).

Now, if you are trying to fit equation (5.10) to a risk of ruin, $RR(b)$, you will fit to find the three parameters that give the best line, as we have done here.

However, if you are trying to fit to risk of drawdown, $RD(b)$, you will only fit for *variableA* and *variableB*. You will *not* fit for the asymptote. Instead, you will assign a value of 1.0 to the asymptote, and fit the other two parameters from there. (You can try to fit for the asymptote as well, but you will merely find it approaches 1.0 with each attempt.)

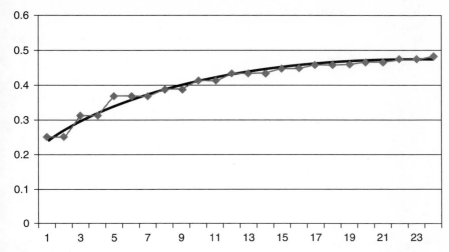

FIGURE 5.6 $RR(.6)$ for 2:1 Coin Toss at $f = .25$ for Both Observed and $RR(.6)$

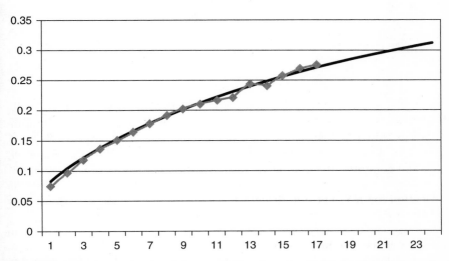

FIGURE 5.7   Data Points and Corresponding Function (5.10) for Our 10 Scenario Real-Life Example

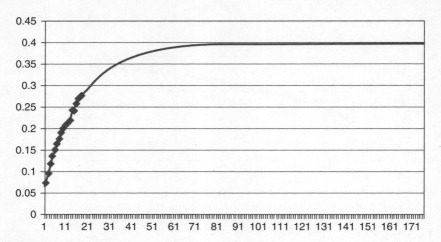

FIGURE 5.8 Data Points and Corresponding Function (5.10) Extended to Show Asymptote in the Function

To confirm the reader's burgeoning uneasiness at this point, consider the following:

In the long-run, the probability of hitting a drawdown (of *any* given magnitude, any b) approaches 1, approaches *certainty* as you continue to trade (that is, as q increases).

$$\lim_{q \to \infty} RD(b, q) = 1.0 \qquad (5.11)$$

This is not as damning a statement as it appears on first reading. Consider the real-world example just alluded to, wherein $RR(.6) = 0.397758$.

Since the probability of hitting a drawdown of any given magnitude (let's say a 99 percent drawdown for argument's sake) approaches 1 as q approaches infinity, yet there is only a roughly 40 percent chance of dropping back to roughly 60 percent of starting equity, we can conclude only that so many q have transpired as to cause the account to have grown by such an amount that a 99 percent drawdown still leaves 60 percent of initial capital.

What we can know, and use, is that (5.05b) can give us a probability of drawdown for a given q. We can use it to learn, for instance, what the probability of drawdown is over, say, the next quarter.

Further, since, we have a GHPR$(f_1 \ldots f_N)$ for each value of (5.05b), we can determine what q we are looking at to reach a specified growth.

$$q = \log_{\text{GHPR}(f_1 \ldots f_N)} TWR(f_1 \ldots f_N) \qquad (3.14a)$$

where: q = the time expected to reach TWR($f_1 \ldots f_N$), which is the target as multiple on our stake

Thus, for example, if my target is a 50 percent return (that is, target TWR = 1.5) and my GHPR from the allocation set I will use in (5.05b) is 1.1, then I will expect it to take q periods, on average, to reach my target TWR:

$$q = \log_{1.1} 1.5 = 4.254164$$

So I would want to consider the $RD(b, 4.254164)$ in this case to be below my threshold probability of such a drawdown.

Notice that we are now considering a risk of drawdown (or ruin) versus that of hitting an upper barrier (that is, target TWR, or u from (5.01)). Deriving q from (3.14a) to use as input to (5.05) is akin to using Feller's classical ruin given in (5.01) only for the more complex case of:

1. A lower barrier, which is not simply just zero.
2. For multiple scenarios, not just the simple binomial gambling sense (of two scenarios).
3. These multiple scenarios are from multiple scenario spectrums, with outcomes occurring simultaneously, with potentially complicated joint probabilities.
4. More important, we are dealing here with geometric growth, not the simple case in Feller where a gambler wins or loses a constant unit with either outcome.

Such analysis—either determining q as the horizon over the next important period (be it a quarter, a year, and so on), or backing into it as the expected number of plays to reach a given target—is how we can determine the portfolio allocation that is growth optimal while remaining within the constraints of an acceptable level of a given drawdown over such a period.

The process detailed in this chapter allows you to maximize geometric returns for a given probability of seeing a given level of drawdown over a given period—which *is* risk. This is something that has either been practiced by intuition by others, with varying degrees of success, or practiced with a metric for risk that is different from drawdown or risk of ruin—often alluded to as *value at risk*.

Essentially, by seeking that highest point (altitude determined as a portfolio's geometric mean HPR or TWR) in the $N + 1$–dimensional landscape of N components, one can mark off those areas within the landscape that cannot be considered for optimal candidates as areas where the probability of risk of ruin or drawdown to a certain point is exceeded.

Returning now to our real-world example of the previous chapter we take our allocations for MktSysA, MktSysB, and MktSysC, and we amend for the greater losses of -150, $-1,000$, and -500 respectively, and we wish to find the maximum GHPR(f_1, f_2, f_3), whereby we do not exceed a 10 percent chance of a 20 percent drawdown ($b = .8$) within the next 12 holding periods (which are in months, so we want the geometric growth optimal allocations to not exceed a 10 percent chance of a 20 percent drawdown in the next year).

Recall we apply a search algorithm (such as the genetic algorithm) to discern that f set that results in the highest GHPR(f_1, f_2, f_3)—or TWR(f_1, f_2, f_3)—yet, at each new, high GHPR((f_1, f_2, f_3) in our search, we look to see if the drawdown constraint has been violated (that is, if the probability of our prescribed drawdown is exceeded within the prescribed time horizon), and if it has, we then assign a value of 0.0 for the GHPR(f_1, f_2, f_3) at the coordinates f_1, f_2, f_3.

In the previous chapter, we found the peak in the 4-D leverage space ($N + 1$) to be at .307, 0.0, .693 for MktSysA, MktSysB, and MktSysC respectively, resulting in a GHPR(.307, 0.0, .693) = 1.249.

Let us assume this is one point in our search, which, as it would be, is a new high GHPR(f_1, f_2, f_3) in our search. Thus, it qualifies as an f set to test versus our prescribed drawdown constraint of "whereby we do not exceed a 10 percent chance of a 20 percent drawdown ($b = .8$) within the next 12 holding periods (months)."

If we exceed a 10 percent probability, then we will set our GHPR(.307, 0.0, .693) = 0 instead of 1.249.

We will now perform (5.05b) in terms of the algorithmic procedure to see if this f set violates our prescribed drawdown constraint. Recall our variables are $N = 3$, $n = 12$. Since our horizon is 12 periods, $q = 12$.

Recall, too, that we want to see if our lower barrier is hit anywhere between period 1 and period q. Thus, think in terms of a tree, starting out at period 1, and expanding to the right as you get to period 12 (that is, q). Thus, we will go to the right, setting a variable i from 1 to q to count off each elapsed time period as we move to the right and the tree expands.

Recall now our joint probabilities table constructed in the previous chapter. This represents the outcomes of each month, binned into a distribution of three components. We know the probability at each bin, and from the N outcomes at each bin ($N = 3$) we can determine the HPR(f_1, f_2, f_3) at each bin. Thus, for the coordinate set .307, 0.0, .693 we have HPR(.307, 0.0, .693)s of:

$i=1$	$i=2$	$i=3$								
MktSysA	MktSysB	MktSysC	Probability	Scenario#	MktSysA HPR(.307)	MktSysB HPR(0)	MktSysC HPR(.693)	Sum	Net HPR (1+Sum-N)	(Net HPR)^P
−$150.00	$253.00	$533.00	0.076923077	1	0.693000	1.000000	1.738738	3.431738	1.431738	1.027991
−$45.33	−$1,000.00	$220.14	0.076923077	2	0.907225	1.000000	1.305114	3.212339	1.212339	1.014922
−$45.33	−$64.43	$220.14	0.153846154	3	0.907225	1.000000	1.305114	3.212339	1.212339	1.030066
$13.00	−$64.43	−$500.00	0.076923077	4	1.026607	1.000000	0.307000	2.333607	0.333607	0.919022
$13.00	−$64.43	$533.00	0.076923077	5	1.026607	1.000000	1.738738	3.765345	1.765345	1.044689
$13.00	$253.00	$220.14	0.076923077	6	1.026607	1.000000	1.305114	3.331721	1.331721	1.022281
$13.00	$253.00	$799.00	0.076923077	7	1.026607	1.000000	2.107414	4.134021	2.134021	1.060042
$13.00	$448.00	$220.14	0.076923077	8	1.026607	1.000000	1.305114	3.331721	1.331721	1.022281
$79.67	−$64.43	−$325.00	0.076923077	9	1.163058	1.000000	0.549550	2.712608	0.712608	0.974273
$79.67	−$64.43	$220.14	0.076923077	10	1.163058	1.000000	1.305114	3.468172	1.468172	1.029980
$79.67	−$64.43	$553.00	0.076923077	11	1.163058	1.000000	1.738738	3.901796	1.901796	1.050689
$136.00	$253.00	$220.14	0.076923077	12	1.278347	1.000000	1.305114	3.583461	1.583461	1.035987
								Geometric Mean HPR=		1.248538088

So from this table, we have the data we need to determine (5.04b):

Scenario#	HPR	Probability
1	1.431738	0.076923077
2	1.212339	0.076923077
3	1.212339	0.153846154
4	0.333607	0.076923077
5	1.765345	0.076923077
6	1.331721	0.076923077
7	2.134021	0.076923077
8	1.331721	0.076923077
9	0.712608	0.076923077
10	1.468172	0.076923077
11	1.901796	0.076923077
12	1.583461	0.076923077

Now, from each i (from 1 to q, as we go from right to left as the tree expands out in possibilities toward our horizon, $q = 12$), we have n^i permutations of these 12 scenarios taken i at a time.

So, where $i = 1$, the leftmost and starting point going from left to right, we have 12 branches ($n^i = 12^1 = 12$). At this stage, each branch is one of the 12 scenarios listed in the previous table.

At the next branch, $i = 2$, each subsequent branch now has each of the n scenarios from the subsequent table appended to it, so we have ($n^i = 12^2 = 144$) branches at $i = 2$, and it appears as follows:

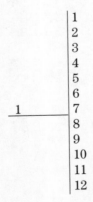

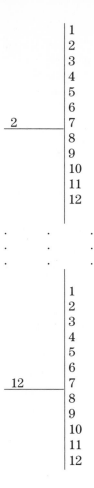

The table shows only the scenario numbers, but recall that for each number, there is a probability assigned to that number, and an HPR(.307,0.0,.693) assigned to it as well.

That branching would continue until $i = q$, or $i = 12$, where we would have $n^i = 12^{12}$ = nearly 9 trillion branches.

Of note here, if the number of branches exceeds 6,250,000 we will simply take 6,250,000 branches at random in determining our calculations at that q. This is the implementation of the first mathematical shortcut technique. Thus, of the nearly 9 trillion branches, we will select 6,250,000 of them at random.

For each of these 6,250,000 branches at $i = q$, $i = 12$, we will calculate its β value, and multiply it times the probability of that branch (which is simply the product of the scenario probabilities at each i on that branch from $i = 1$ to q).

Thus, assume we randomly had, as one of our 6,250,000 branches, the branch comprised of the following scenario numbers:

1, 6, 11, 7, 9, 1, 6, 9, 2, 3, 1, 5

We could arrange this to appear as follows:

$i =$	1	2	3	4	5	6
scenario#	1	6	11	7	9	1
Corresponding HPR	1.431738	1.331721	1.901796	2.134021	0.712608	1.431738
Probability	0.07692	0.07692	0.07692	0.07692	0.07692	0.07692

$i =$	7	8	9	10	11	12
scenario#	6	9	2	3	1	5
Corresponding HPR	1.33172	0.712608	1.21234	1.212339	1.431738	1.765345
Probability	0.07692	0.07692	0.07692	0.15385	0.07692	0.07692

This represents one value for k (in $k =$ the minimum of n^q or 6,250,000), Remember, we are looking for a β value for this k, which is:

$$\text{int}\left(\frac{\sum_{i=1}^{q}\left(\min\left(1.0, \left(\prod_{t=0}^{i-1} HPR(f_1 \ldots f_N)_t\right)\right) * HPR(f_1 \ldots f_N)_i - b\right)}{\sum_{i=1}^{q}\left|\left(\min\left(1.0, \left(\prod_{t=0}^{i-1} HPR(f_1 \ldots f_N)_t\right)\right) * HPR(f_1 \ldots f_N)_i - b\right)\right|}\right)$$

in (5.05b). Further recall we will multiply this β value for this k times the sum of its probabilities for this k:

$$\prod_{i=1}^{q} Prob_{k,i}$$

in (5.05b). If we multiply the cells in the probability row together from the above table, we get the product 8.5844E-14, a very small number indeed, and thus you can begin to see how floating point precision can wreak a degree of havoc in our calculations!

We continue now calculating this horizontal run, along this branch of q data points. Note that we have a row entitled "HPR Products." This is simply the minimum of the previous running product of HPRs up to that

$q - 1$ HPR Product, or 1, consistent with our formula since we are looking at drawdown here, not at risk of ruin.

$i =$	1	2	3	4	5	6
scenario#	1	6	11	7	9	1
Corresponding HPR	1.43174	1.33172	1.90180	2.13402	0.71261	1.43174
Probability	0.07692	0.07692	0.07692	0.07692	0.07692	0.07692
HPR Products	1.00000	1.00000	1.00000	1.00000	0.71261	1.00000
HPR Products-b (b=.8)	0.20000	0.20000	0.20000	0.20000	−0.08739	0.20000
Abs(HPR Products-b)	0.20000	0.20000	0.20000	0.20000	0.08739	0.20000

$i =$	7	8	9	10	11	q 12	
scenario#	6	9	2	3	1	5	
Corresponding HPR	1.331721	0.712608	1.212339	1.212339	1.431738	1.765345	Product 8.6E-14
Probability	0.076923	0.076923	0.076923	0.153846	0.076923	0.076923	
HPR Products	1	0.712608	0.863922	1	1	1	Sums
HPR Products-b (b=.8)	0.2	−0.087392	0.063922	0.2	0.2	0.2	1.68914
Abs(HPR Products-b)	0.2	0.087392	0.063922	0.2	0.2	0.2	2.03871

Just below each HPR Products cell, there is the value of that HPR Product minus b, or minus .8. This is so we may see if we have touched the lower absorbing barrier (and if we have, the value in this row would be negative).

Beneath that, we have the absolute value of the HPR Product minus b row, which gives us only positive values.

Next, we sum up both of these rows, the HPR Products minus b row, and the absolute value of that row.

We then divide, with the absolute value in the denominator:

$$1.68914/2.03871 = 0.82853427$$

Finally, take the integer of this value to give us our β value for this k, this row:

$$\text{int}(0.82853427) = 0$$

thus, for this k, this row:

$$\beta_k = 0$$

Suppose instead of a 20 percent drawdown (that is, $b = .8$), we were looking at a 30 percent drawdown ($b = .7$); we would have had the following instead:

$i =$	1	2	3	4	5	6
scenario#	1	6	11	7	9	1
Corresponding HPR	1.43174	1.33172	1.90180	2.13402	0.71261	1.43174
Probability	0.07692	0.07692	0.07692	0.07692	0.07692	0.07692
HPR Products	1.00000	1.00000	1.00000	1.00000	0.71261	1.00000
HPR Products-b (b=.7)	0.30000	0.30000	0.30000	0.30000	0.01261	0.30000
Abs(HPR Products-b)	0.30000	0.30000	0.30000	0.30000	0.01261	0.30000

						q	
$i =$	7	8	9	10	11	12	
scenario#	6	9	2	3	1	5	
Corresponding HPR	1.331721	0.712608	1.212339	1.212339	1.431738	1.765345	Product
Probability	0.076923	0.076923	0.076923	0.153846	0.076923	0.076923	8.6E-14
HPR Products	1	0.712608	0.863922	1	1	1	Sums
HPR Products-b (b=.7)	0.3	0.012608	0.163922	0.3	0.3	0.3	2.88914
Abs(HPR Products-b)	0.3	0.012608	0.163922	0.3	0.3	0.3	2.88914

Summing up both of these rows, the HPR Products minus b row, and the absolute value of that row, then dividing, with the absolute value in the denominator:

$$2.88914/2.88914 = 1$$

And finally, take the integer of this value to give us our β value for this k, this row:

$$int(1) = 1$$

In other words, if ruin was defined as a 30 percent drawdown, this k row would *not* have seen ruin.

Next, for all of our 6,250,000 rows here, we must multiply each β value by the probability of that k node. Recall earlier the probability of this was determined to be 8.5844E-14. So if we were looking at a 30 percent drawdown, we would multiply our β value of 1 for this k by 8.5844E-14 to obtain a result of 8.5844E-14. If we were looking at a 20 percent drawdown, our β value is 0, and multiplying this by 8.5844E-14 still results in 0.

We now add together all of these results (we will either have n^q of them, or 6,250,000, whichever is the lesser) for all of these rows, and the result will then be divided by the sum of all probabilities used in all the rows we have calculated over (n^q or 6,250,000, whichever is the lesser). Note a

k^{th} probability is added to the sum of the probabilities in the denominator whether the β_k value was 0 or not.

Finally, this resultant product of division of all the probability-weighted β values of each k, divided by the sum of the probabilities for each k, is subtracted from 1 to give us our probability of drawdown.

In doing so, if we perform all 6,250,000 rows, we find indeed that our drawdown constraint was violated at the f coordinates of .307,0.0,.693 and we therefore set GHPR(.307, 0.0, .693) = 0 instead of 1.249, and continue on with our search.

Eventually, we find the peak at the coordinates .191, .007, .165 that results in the highest GHPR(f_1, f_2, f_3) without violating our prescribed drawdown constraint of no more than a 10 percent chance of a 20 percent drawdown over the next 12 periods (months) and results in the following allocations:

MktSysA	0.191	$786.31
MktSysB	0.007	$152,431.31
MktSysC	0.165	$3,035.23

and a GHPR(.191, .007, .165) of 1.087 and an $RD(0.8)$ of 9.8 percent out to 12 periods. This indicates a 9.8 percent chance of a 20 percent drawdown over the next 12 months.

Note that since we are using monthly data, the drawdown is calculated using monthly data; quite possibly, the drawdown, on a day-to-day basis, can exceed what we are considering here. The drawdown we are operating against in this example is the probability therefore of a drawdown based on monthly data.

There you have it in 137 pages—where we are and how we got here in terms of geometric mean maximization.

MATHEMATICAL ADDENDUM TO PART II: THE MULTIPLE COMPONENT CASE

Conditional Probabilities

We have discussed the concept of a "horizontal run," a simultaneous set of given outcomes of the various scenario sets, followed by subsequent outcomes of given scenario sets, expressed as:

$$Prob_{k,1} * Prob_{k,2} * \cdots * Prob_{k,q} = p_k$$

In the chapter, we simply assumed independence of the $Prob_{k,?}$ and mentioned that in the absence of independence, other formulas should be used. These shall be provided now.

Consider the notion of "conditional probability," the probability that an event occurs given that a given event's occurrence preceded it—specifically as referred here, say, the probability of $Prob_{k,2}$ occurring given that $Prob_{k,1}$ has occurred. This is expressed as:

$$P(Prob_{k,2}|Prob_{k,1})$$

And we can state that:

$$P(Prob_{k,2}|Prob_{k,1}) = P(Prob_{k,1}, \ Prob_{k,2})/P(Prob_{k,1})$$

where: $P(Prob_{k,1}, \ Prob_{k,2}) =$ the joint or compound probability that $Prob_{k,1}$ and $Prob_{k,2}$ occur

From this, we obtain what is referred to as the *General Law of Compound Probability* (sometimes referred to as the *Multiplication Theorem*) and is used to discern our p_k values:

$$p_k = P(Prob_{k,1}, \ Prob_{k,2}, \cdots Prob_{k,q}) = P(Prob_{k,1}) * P(Prob_{k,2}|Prob_{k,1})*$$
$$P(Prob_{k,3}|Prob_{k,1}, \ Prob_{k,2}) * \cdots * P(Prob_{k,q}|Prob_{k,1}, \ Prob_{k,2}, \cdots Prob_{k,q-1})$$

The case of the outcomes being independent, as is (often justifiably, given the empirical market data) used in this chapter, is considered a special case where the Law of Compound Probability reduces to:

$$p_k = P(Prob_{k,1}, \ Prob_{k,2}, \ldots Prob_{k,q}) = Prob_{k,1} * Prob_{k,2} * \ldots * Prob_{k,q}$$

PART III

The Leverage Space Praxis

CHAPTER 6

A Framework to Satisfy Both Economic Theory and Portfolio Managers

T hus far, we have seen how to determine an optimal f value. We've expounded upon it so that we are now able to use a single equation to determine it for any number of scenarios (outcomes) for innumerable games played simultaneously (portfolio components traded) or for the single-game case.

We have also studied the nature of the curve in the single-component case, which extrapolates out to whatever axis a component resides on in the multiple-component case.

We have seen that this is important, because it applies to us unavoidably and because we are at some point on that curve, that $N+1$–dimensional surface. We are likely to be moving along it, unwittingly, with the passage of holding periods, oblivious to what is happening to us and how we might harness it.

In addition, we have introduced the notion of drawdown as a risk metric, and constructed an algorithmic means to determine both it and the probability of ruin or drawdown. We have seen how these progress asymptotically as the number of plays (holding periods) increases.

Taken together, we have managed to construct a portfolio model that is superior to those that have been widely practiced for half a century. As we have seen, this model is superior for the following four reasons:

1. Risk is defined as *drawdown*, not variance in returns.
2. The model is valid for *any* distributional form; *fat tails* are addressed.

3. The Leverage Space Model is about *leverage*, which is not addressed in the traditional models.

4. The fallacy and danger of *correlation* is eliminated.

Finally, we have seen, step by step, how to perform the algorithms to accomplish these ends.

The planet is small. The jets are fast. Back in Tokyo I am having lunch, and Hiro stirs the pot with something I had only marginally had bubbling in my head for the past few years.

"You know," Hiro started, "What is really needed is to be able to maximize not profit, but rather the probability of being profitable by a certain point in time. That's what fund managers and traders are really up against—not making tons of money, but *making* money."

It knocked me over because I knew, suddenly, instantly, he was absolutely, undeniably right. I knew when Hiro spoke those words, this path of reasoning, that of "profit maximization" *as a criterion*, a thread of thought nearly three centuries in distillation, had just received an exogenous shock that would forever alter how I looked at it. I knew this because I could see exactly what he was asking in a *context*, and that the solution was *not* enigmatic or elusive. I knew that this "context" was *geometric mean maximization*, because there are optimal, mathematical answers therein.

Hit the brakes. Cut the wheel. I shall now extricate myself from the very box I have built around myself like a prison regarding geometric mean maximization.

At the beginning of Chapter 1, I stated, "To this point in time, the notion of geometric mean maximization has been a *criterion*. . . ." However, "Our criterion is rarely growth-optimality. Yet growth optimality is the criterion that is solved mathematically. Mathematics, devoid of human propensities, proclivities, and predilections, can readily arrive at a clean, 'optimal' point. As such, it provides a framework for us to satisfy our seemingly labyrinthine appetites."

Thus far, we have been discussing matters in terms of raw gains and losses, whether we are speaking of them in a multiplicative manner (as in GHPRs or TWRs) or in a pure arithmetic manner (as with Mathematical Expectation). Our discussion has thus far been absent the *effect* of these gains or losses on the investor. We have looked at things in the sense of assuming the investor prefers gains and his criterion has simply been to maximize his gains. Mathematically, this is a straightforward problem to solve. Arguably, it should be the only criterion for investors (but in the real world the investor is the customer, and his complex desires become a constraint upon the portfolio manager to satisfy; it does not, whatever the basis of the customer's desires, mathematically legitimize them). Further, regardless of the desires of man as a singular, aggregated entity, or a solo individual, the mathematics and the landscape of growth optimality (ripped in portions by "risk") remain unaffected, the ineluctable coordinates of each investor still having him on that surface and affected by his immediate location thereon.

We now seek to satisfy what the *human psyche prefers*, as opposed to merely raw gains. In other words, the discipline of portfolio management, the discipline of money management, of "position sizing," has been one of heretofore seeking to maximize gains within a given (however nebulous) "risk" constraint. Rather than seeking to maximize gains, we shall seek to maximize what the human psyche prefers (what the customers of fund managers prefer) with respect to risk (drawdown, plus or replaced by any other risk-metric constraints).

People do not make decisions based on maximizing expected values—what we call the Mathematical Expectation. Instead, there is a seemingly pathological element to their decision making, which so-called Economic Theory has tried to explain.

The reason we want to satisfy this "seemingly pathological element," this "labyrinthine appetite," is because the portfolio manager's customers are not interested in maximizing gains as their criterion. Those customers' seemingly pathological criteria *are* often labyrinthine, with numerous criteria interwoven among themselves and, at times, competing with themselves.

Return now back to the paradox posited by Nicolaus Bernoulli, Daniel's cousin, in Chapter 1 (equation (1.01)). The paradox there was presented as a question: "What would you pay to enter a game with an infinite mathematical expectation as a payoff to you?"

Our story thus far has seen two separate lines of reasoning. We've seen the thread of geometric mean maximization woven throughout the story. We've also seen how, starting in the 1950s, the concept of Modern Portfolio Theory has surfaced and gained widespread acceptance.

This third line of reasoning, introduced by the famous letter of Nicolaus I Bernoulli to Pierre Raymond de Montmort in 1713 (wherein this paradox arises), rejoins our story. This third thread of reasoning is particularly fascinating, for it attempts to explain this seemingly pathological nature of human beings.

In 1728, in private correspondence with Nicolaus Bernoulli, Gabriel Cramer, another Swiss mathematician, proposed a solution to the paradox Nicolaus Bernoulli raised in his 1713 letter to Pierre Raymond de Montmort. Cramer argues that every subsequent gain at each subsequent toss matters less and less to the beneficiary.

Cramer is very close to the notion Daniel Bernoulli will propose. In 1738, in Daniel Bournoulli's *Specimen theoriae novae de mensura sortis* or *Exposition of a New Theory on the Measurement of Risk*, he called this the *St. Petersburg Paradox* (this is the first time we see this paradox referred to by that name). Bernoulli's 1738 publication, if you will recall from Chapter 1, also happens to be the first known recording of the notion of geometric mean maximization. In it, Bernoulli proposed that a mathematical function should be used to correct the expected value, and he is credited with the first formalization of the notion of "marginal utility," as well as the notion of expected utility theory itself.

In effect, the formula for Expected Utility is the same as that of Mathematical Expectation, but the outcomes are expressed in terms of the utility afforded by the outcomes. Mathematically, Expected Utility (EU):

$$EU = \sum_{i=1}^{n} (P_i * U(A_i)) \tag{6.01}$$

where: P_i = the probability associated with the ith outcome
A_i = the result of the ith outcome
$U()$ = the utility function
n = the total number of possible outcomes

Essentially, Expected Utility (EU) is the mathematical expectation (ME) of utility, and utility is a function of the value of an outcome. Often, people's "utility functions" are considered "lognormal," that is, the marginal increase in utility is ever less, is lognormal. A win of 100 units, to a man with a stake of 100 units, is worth more, in terms of utility gained, than a win of 100 units to a man with 1,000,000 units. That's one way to view the idea of why people will trade in quantity relative to the size of their stake.

In brief, the Expected Utility Theorem states that people will size up wagers based upon mathematical relations (the $U(A_i)$ functions in equation (6.01)), which takes into account not only the size of a payout and the probabilities of occurrence (that is, the basic Mathematical Expectation, ME) but also their own, personal risk aversion as a function of how much wealth they already have. It is, therefore, a considerably more refined theory than simply predicting that choices will be made based on the highest Mathematical Expectation.

The comparison of simply maximizing expected value to maximizing expected utility gave rise to a new discipline, known as "Economic Theory." There are many names along the evolution of Economic Theory; we're merely creating a thumbnail sketch for where Economic Theory and our story of geometric mean maximization meet in terms of application to relative trading quantities.

In 1944, John von Neumann and Oskar Morgenstern reinterpreted the Expected Utility Theorem and presented an axiomatization of it. The outgrowth of their 1944 work is often looked upon as the cornerstone of "Game Theory."[1] In addition to their Axiomatic Utility Theory presented therein (which led to the widespread adoption of utility theory in the field of economics), this 1944 work discusses two-person, zero-sum games and describes the idea of a cooperative game, with transferable utility, its coalitional form and its von Neumann-Morgenstern stable sets.

These notions spawned an explosion in the following decades of a litany of great minds with applications in biology, sociology, computer science, warfare, politics, and a cornucopia of other sciences, the list of people and concepts requiring volumes to adequately catalogue.

However, we're following a storyline here, and our storyline is not about Game Theory. Our storyline is about Economic Theory meeting up with geometric mean maximization. But Economic Theory, and its elaborate history, cannot even be scratched without mention of the seminal genius of Game Theory, John von Neumann and (with Oskar Morgenstern) his 1944 work on Game Theory that incorporated Expected Utility theory into an axiomatized articulation.

In 1966, Robert MacArthur, an ecologist, and biologist Eric Pianka, addressed the concept of foraging behavior, a long-running concern in ecology, with "On the optimal use of a patchy environment" (MacArthur and Pianka 1966), which presents what is known as "Optimal Foraging Theory."

Optimal Foraging Theory states that organisms forage in a manner so as to maximize their energy intake per unit of time. Organisms (including primates, such as human beings) behave in such a way as to find, obtain, and consume food containing the most calories while expending the least amount of time (calories) possible in doing so.

Though not presented as an economic theory, its relationship to economic theory of the coming decades would be so close that this Optimal Foraging Theory deserves special mention in this brief, whirlwind tour of Economic Theory.

---

[1]In truth, the term "Game Theory" was quite possibly coined in the 1944 work. However, the notions of Game Theory date at least as far back as sometime in the first five centuries A.D., where in the *Talmud* we find seemingly contradictory recommendations for what a deceased man should leave his three wives, proposing three different divisions based on different values of his estate! Talmudic scholars have scratched their heads at this one for a good 15 centuries. In 1985, it was recognized that the *Talmud* anticipates the modern theory of cooperative games. Each solution it is shown, corresponds to the nucleolus of an apposite defined game (Aumann and Maschler 1985).

In 1979, Daniel Kahneman and Amos Tversky proposed what is called "Prospect Theory," also known as "Loss-Aversion Theory." Starting with how people respond to empirical evidence pertaining to choices, and the fact that this data often flies in the face of Expected Utility Theory, Kahneman and Tversky's work presents a psychologically realistic alternative to Expected Utility Theory consistent with observed behavior.

To see an example of Prospect Theory in action, suppose a man wants to take his wife to a play. He might balk at paying 200 units for a single ticket, but he would happily pay 100 units for each ticket, and so he buys two tickets for a total of 200 units.

Now suppose he loses his two tickets. Empirical evidence shows that the man will buy two more tickets at 100 units apiece. He now has two tickets that he paid 400 units total for.

Similarly, when he made his first visit to the ticket booth, had those same tickets been on sale for only 50 units, he would not have purchased four of them for a total of 200 units. Rather, he would have purchased only two.

Prospect Theory differs from Expected Utility Theory in a number ways. For one thing, Prospect Theory treats preferences as a function of "weights," and it assumes that these weights do not always correspond to probabilities. Furthermore, Prospect Theory proposes that these weights tend to overweight small probabilities and underweight moderate and high probabilities.

Prospect Theory also replaces the notion of "utility" with "value." Whereas utility is usually defined only in terms of net wealth, value is defined in terms of gains and losses—deviations from a *reference point*. The *value function* has a different shape for gains and losses. For losses, we find it tends to be convex and relatively steep, while for gains it tends to be concave and not quite so steep.

Mathematically, *Prospect Theory Expected Value (PTEV)*:

$$PTEV = \sum_{i=1}^{n} (W(P_i) * V(A_i)) \tag{6.02}$$

where: P_i = the probability associated with the ith outcome
A_i = the result of the ith outcome
$V()$ = the value function (in lieu of Expected Utility Theory's Utility function)
$W()$ = the weighting function
n = the total number of possible outcomes

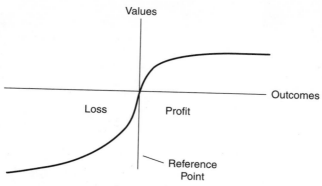

FIGURE 6.1 Prospect Theory Expected Value (*PTEV*)

Graphically, PTEV tends to the shape shown in Figure 6.1.

Prospect Theory explains certain mathematically inexplicable behaviors in human beings, such as the "Reflection Effect," wherein most people would choose a certain gain of 25 units over a one-third chance of gaining 75 units. At the same time, they would choose a one-third chance of losing 75 units (and two-thirds chance of losing nothing) over a certain loss of 25 units.

There is also a certain behavioral characteristic in humans referred to in Prospect Theory as the "Framing Effect." This is a change of preferences between options as a function of the variation of "frames," a variation of the formulation of the problem. Is the glass half full or half empty?

For example, a problem can be presented as a gain ($^3/_4$ of the crop can be saved) or as a loss ($^1/_4$ of the crop will be ruined). In the former, human beings tend to adopt a gain frame, which generally leads to risk-aversion. In the latter human beings tend to adopt a loss frame, generally leading to behavior that is risk seeking.

Prospect Theory predicts both the Reflection and the Framing effects in the "S" shape of the PTEV function. It is concave for gains indicating risk aversion, and it is convex for losses indicating risk seeking.

Our whirlwind tour of the thread of Economic Theory finally takes us to 2008, when Rose McDermott, James Fowler, and Oleg Smirnov make the connection between Optimal Foraging Theory and Prospect Theory, pointing out that survival thresholds might be responsible for human attitudes toward risk.

Hiro's words resonate with this. People want to be profitable, they want to show "a profit," the magnitude of which is a distant secondary concern versus not showing a profit.

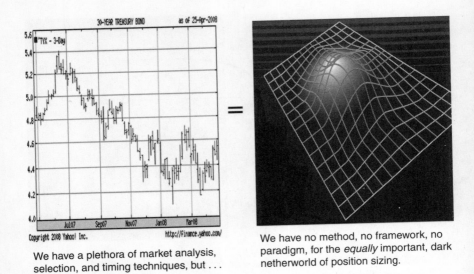

We have a plethora of market analysis, selection, and timing techniques, but . . .

We have no method, no framework, no paradigm, for the *equally* important, dark netherworld of position sizing.

FIGURE 6.2 Market Analysis and Position Sizing (Both Equally Necessary)

Human beings want to have beans to eat, versus having no beans at all. Having mountains of beans in the future is not nearly as important as having *some* beans *today*.

The portfolio manager wants to show his clients a profit as opposed to a loss, far more so than he wants to show them a large profit.

And the clients want that, too.

The *human psyche prefers* to be happy, to be satisfied, but not necessarily satiated. "Satiation," it appears, does not rise to the level of a "drive" in human impulse. We see this with Prospect Theory and Optimal Foraging Theory. People act seemingly irrationally, in a mathematical sense, but it is not at all irrational considering the evolutionary, hard-wired reasons that people behave that way. It also explains the near-universal, visceral reaction I have received for a couple of decades regarding geometric mean maximization as a criterion.

You can lead a horse to water, but you can't teach him the backstroke.

Regardless of the desires of man as a singular, aggregated entity, or a solo individual, the mathematics and the landscape of growth optimality (ripped in portions by "risk") remains unaffected, the ineluctable coordinates of each investor still having him on that surface and affected by his immediate location thereon, as depicted in Figure 6.2.

We have seen in this text that even winning systems can lose, as we witness in the 2:1 coin toss situation, wherein $f > .5$ loses with certainty as we continue to play, *even in a cash account.*

If we simply examine three separate points in that landscape, we can clearly see why quantity trumps timing and selection. If I happen to be at the peak (call this Point 1) of the terrain in the $N+1$–dimensional landscape, for a goodly number of periods, I am likely to make more than I could imagine. At Point 2, I am near the $0,0\ldots0$ point in the landscape. I make very little, compared to Point 1, but more likely than not, my drawdowns are quite tolerable. At Point 3, I am beyond the point where the landscape dips to where it guarantees I lose in the long run on *any* of the N axes. In other words, if I am wrong on only one axis, the entire thing will lose with certainty, contrary to the mean-variance delusion, and we're *still* talking about being in a cash account. I thus have N winning propositions, the aggregate is a total loss, and only because I had my quantity wrong on 1 of the N components.

We have seen how Modern Portfolio Theory fails us entirely in at least four ways. We have also seen how the degree of profitability, as well as drawdowns, are profoundly dictated by our location on the landscape versus other locations.

Clearly, position sizing is equally as important as your market analysis, timing, and selection. I hope I have demonstrated that the Leverage Space Portfolio Model is superior, as a portfolio model, to those provided by Modern Portfolio Theory.

Just as you wouldn't want to trade without your charts, analysis, and other timing tools, you don't want to suffer the consequences of being ignorant of the fact that this dark netherworld of quantity unwittingly works against you.

This is especially true when, as I hope I have demonstrated, the quantity you have on is at least half of what affects you (though, I contend it is 100 percent). Additionally, quantity is the *only* thing you have complete control over.

This dark netherworld of leverage space that we are automatically in, and the palate of human beings, illuminated through economic theory, is easily reconciled.

And this reconciliation changes things.

Suppose you are engaged in two multiple, simultaneous 2:1 coin toss games. Further, assume you are oblivious to the fact that you are somewhere on the $N+1$–dimensional surface of leverage space, and of the effects upon you therefrom.

Let's say that you decide, based on your gut, to initially allocate one bet for every 5 units to each game in your stake of 100 units. Thus, you initially make 20 1-unit bets on the one coin toss, and make 20 1-unit bets on the other 1-coin toss occurring simultaneously. We can determine where you are in the 3D ($N + 1$)–dimensional landscape here as .2,.2, putting you "just to the left" of the optimal .23,.23 point (although you are oblivious to this).

However, that was your *initial* allocation. Suppose your game plan calls for you to maintain 20 1-unit bets toward each game, regardless of the outcomes to that point.

With each play we can determine, from what is in your stake, what your coordinates are in the $N+1$–dimensional landscape. We expect you to make money, on average, given the positive expectation. Thus, as the stake grows, we would likely see your coordinates migrate from .2,.2 toward 0,0. In so doing, we could further expect the effects of being more and more to the left of the peak, in terms of the nature of the curve, to affect you (although you witness its effect, you are unaware that it is a result of your position on the surface).

Notice that you are not using the concept of leverage space, but you are in it, and it is working upon you. What you are experiencing is a *migration function* through leverage space.

Everything we have discussed about leverage space and geometric mean maximization holds true, and you *are* experiencing it along your migratory path through it. Even so, although you are trading in a constant amount as you are in this game, you are not seeking to maximize geometric growth. Of course, with each play you are still on the landscape, migrating around on it, with the consequences and payoffs of your current location thereon affecting you.

This was a case of being oblivious to leverage space, and an inadvertent migration function.

Now, however, if we look at leverage space not as a portfolio model and not with geometric mean maximization as our criterion, but rather, with a different criterion, we can harness the effect of leverage space to map out a migration function through it to *satisfy* our "seemingly pathological human psyches."

Since you are ineluctably at some f coordinate set, then, unless you are trading, consciously, on a fixed fractional basis, you are thus ineluctably moving about, migrating, through the landscape.

In other words, the peak in leverage space, juxtaposed to risk (drawdown) is *not* our criterion. Instead, we seek to create a function to migrate through leverage space in a manner that satisfies our criterion. Leverage space is the context, the "map," that we use to create this criterion-satisfying function within. With this paradigm, we no longer need to operate blindly in the dark netherworld that is so riddled with heuristics, misinformation, and what is essentially mere alchemy (such as "never risk more than 1 percent/2 percent" rules, half Kelly, Modern Portfolio Theory, Capital Asset Pricing Model, and so on). Why would anybody want to operate blindly through it? Would you want to trade without the inputs that you presently use for your trading decisions, making such trading decisions in the dark?

The evolution of those heuristics, where they seem to have value, becomes evident when viewed through the lens of this framework.

In the beginning of Chapter 1, it was pointed out that mathematics, which allows us to "readily arrive at a clean, 'optimal' point ... provides a framework for us to satisfy our seemingly labyrinthine appetites."

In other words, we can construct our framework, our context, mathematically. Our appetites, however, are not for the "mathematically" optimal (that is, the geometric growth optimal). Rather, the context, the framework, allows us a view, a means to achieve what we want and what our appetites call for. It gives us a context to operate within. Every money management strategy, every so-called position sizing, methodology, every gambling progression, is a migration function, and every portfolio allocation (by whatever portfolio model) can be located within this framework. Its path of migration can be discerned, the benefits and consequences elucidated in this context.

In recent years, others have offered up differing means of determining optimal trading quantities. Every one of them is, in effect, an ineluctable migration function, moving about ineluctable coordinates in leverage space (and deriving the benefits and paying the consequences of being at those coordinates)—however oblivious the techniques are to this phenomenon. Geometric mean maximization to this point is a prelude; it is a foundation, providing a mere framework, a description of the landscape of the netherworld you reside in, and that affects you as much as your skills of analysis, timing, and selection do. Yes, you could use it as a criterion (growth optimality, seeking that highest point within the landscape, your migration function having you remain at that point interminably). Absent knowing that you are on a curve, without knowing the peak of that curve—that is, the optimal point—or the bounds of 0 and 1 to the curve, there *is* no "context" and you cannot know where you are, or what you are doing, without having the landmark of the peak to navigate from, and the scope of the landscape.

The framework is important because, as I have said, it allows us to examine the tradeoffs in our behavior in terms of quantity, which is the dark, undefined netherworld side of trading where little is known (which is why I pursued finding out about it so vigorously). As charts give us a framework for technical analysis, we have (finally) a framework for working with this necessary netherworld of quantity.

This is the *dénouement* of the Leverage Space Model itself (of all portfolio models, for that matter)—using it as a framework, as a tool wherein all strategies pertaining to quantity can be examined, and examined in a context that makes *sense* to us. Precisely because it *is* a framework (although it started out as a superior portfolio model, it is much more than

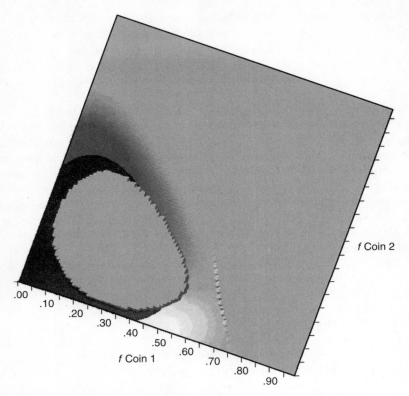

FIGURE 6.3   Real-World, Two-Component Example Seen from Above

that), we can now look into some truly interesting and gratifying applications of it.

With this framework, we now can go about satisfying that which the human psyche prefers (such as what a fund manager's customers prefer), however seemingly pathological, and we can do this in a way that is consistent with the precepts of Economic Theory, which explain this seeming pathological element, dispelling it. We accomplish this via functions that have us navigate viable portions of the landscape to accomplish what we determine is our criterion. Figure 6.3 shows a two-component example landscape.

Thus, in seeking methods to reconcile portfolio management strategies and economic theory, we seek migration functions, within the framework, as opposed to the atavistic notion of "portfolio models," which are static, inaccurate at modeling the world you operate in, and do not address the desires of the investor elucidated in economic theories. See Figure 6.4.

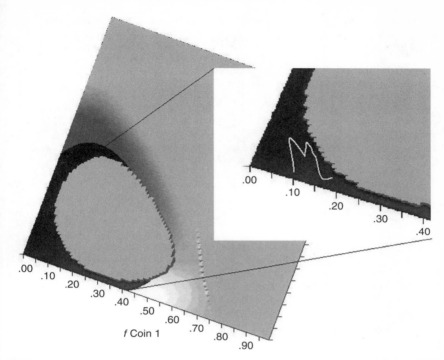

FIGURE 6.4 Real-World, Two-Component Example with a Migration Path within the Framework

The notion of portfolio models is a twentieth-century one. I have no interest in them. Rather, as I am attempting to demonstrate, "Frameworks" give us the instrument we need to accomplish the specific ends we seek. Frameworks provide us with a means of viewing something, a mathematically formulated lens of what is occurring in front of us, rather than a portfolio model, per se.

The desiccated old models are not only irrelevant, they have never shed any light on the dark netherworld regarding quantity. They burden and disable the mind. The Leverage Space Model—when viewed as a framework—allows us far more fluid and mercurial solutions for achieving our specific goals.

It has been said that successful investing is perhaps 99 percent about controlling risks and 1 percent about maximizing the profit potential of an investment opportunity.

However, the predicate of "maximizing the profit potential of an investment opportunity" is simply not true. People tend to place the degree of profitability at a distant second to profitability itself, treating the degree of profitability as an afterthought.

By way of example, we could ask just where it is in the managed money industry that performance fees are actually staggered by *degrees* of performance.

Let us look at managed futures, whereby I might have a schedule for performance fees along the lines of:

Return	Percentage Performance Fee
<2%	0%
2%–5%	1%
5%–10%	5%
10%–20%	20%
20%>	25%

Have you ever seen such a progression of management fees based on performance? If people really *were* concerned with profitability, such a scheme would be ubiquitous. Rather, we see something like "20 percent of new high equity," regardless of the degree of new high equity.

In other words—people *want* that new high equity and they don't care so much about the degree of it. They want to be profitable.

What people desire (on the upside) has been murky, amorphous, and undefined. They don't know what they want on the upside; they will tell you several things, and that will also vary from individual to individual. Yet, no one has articulated what people *really* want. It is not, except in the rarest of cases, to maximize profits even *with* respect to risk. I have not encountered this apocryphal character.

Worse yet, what they fear, too, has been murky, amorphous, and undefined. Variance? (Excepting those who *are* benchmarked to that, and compensated about it.) Drawdown? How do you quantify that?

We *have* looked at the risk side of the risk-reward juxtaposition that is innate to portfolio models, and we have managed to quantify risk in terms of drawdown, rather than merely variance in returns.

In the next chapter, we will redefine the reward aspect as well. In addition, we will show how to use our results in real-world, day-to-day applications via migration functions, rather than having our ideas simply sizzling away on dry ice, frozen in the darkened corners of a figurative laboratory with attainable real-world application out of reach.

I would, therefore, amend the predicate "and 1 percent about maximizing the profit potential of an investment opportunity" to be "and 1 percent about just being profitable—to any degree—an investment opportunity."

Let us return now to the notion of what my friend Hiro said about the necessity of a means of maximizing the probability of being profitable. It is perfectly congruent with Prospect Theory and perfectly congruent with Optimal Foraging Theory. Of course, this is what has been needed, which Hiro so clearly illuminated for me.

Modern Portfolio Theory doesn't give us this. As we've seen, it is likely to just get us unwittingly into trouble. We leave portfolio models in the past now, and instead adopt the concept of a framework and the requisite migration functions to achieve the specific ends we seek through the framework.

CHAPTER 7

Maximizing the Probability of Profit

G eometric mean maximization requires small anti-Martingale type progressions, which trade in quantity with respect to account size, increasing trading quantity as equity increases. They are *profit* maximizers, and hence have an equity curve that is mostly flat at best for very long stretches of time; they tend to see enormous and rapid growth, such that one can see that exponential growth has occurred by the right-hand side of the equity curve.

On the other hand, in maximizing the *probability of profit* (*PP*), one is not concerned with geometric growth, nor even with smoothness in an equity curve, but rather that at some future point (some "horizon" defined as a designated number of holding periods from the present one) the equity curve will be above where it is today, plus some prescribed amount, with the highest probability. This requires a Martingale or small Martingale progression.

Typically, a Martingale doubles the bet size with each losing bet. As soon as the losing streak is broken, a one-unit gain is realized. The downside is that as the losing streak continues, the bet sizes double with each losing play, and eventually the required bet size is unachievable.[1]

---

[1]Recall the axiom posited in the Introduction to this text: *In a game with a negative ME (for instance, most gambling games) the probability of going broke approaches certainty as you continue to play.* Note that even in a Martingale progression (with a guarantee of making one unit, *eventually*), if such a game, with no minimum bet size or table limits, could be discovered, and if we pick an arbitrary time, an arbitrary q, to look at our player's stake, we would expect our player to be

Typically then, Martingale and small Martingale-type systems suffer from larger drawdown than their opposing counterparts, which trade in quantity relative to account size, such as geometric mean maximization strategies.

In Chapter 5 we saw a means of quantifying drawdown, allowing us to now use the constraint of drawdown as our risk metric,[2] such that we may now employ a Martingale-style approach within the leverage space terrain—without the corresponding risk of larger drawdown that is usually inherent in such an approach.[3]

We will now demonstrate a procedure for a small Martingale progression for capitalizing portfolio components, which seeks to maximize the

---

down, on average, by the mathematical expectation times how much he has bet to this point, q. However, if we allow the gambler to bet *à la* Martingale and to quit as soon as he shows a profit, he is guaranteed this profit as the length of the game approaches infinity (which assumes our player has either an infinitely large initial stake, and/or wagers in infinitely small size for a unit). However, at any arbitrary $0 < q < x$ where x is the point of being profitable, we expect him to be losing by an amount equal to the mathematical expectation times how much he has bet to this point, q. After such a point, $x <= q < \infty$, our player, now up one unit, stands and watches the game, no longer wagering. Arguably, this is an example of a negative expectation game that is made into a winner via its migration path as the length of the game approaches infinity—hence the caveat regarding the probability of going broke in a negative expectation game approaching certainty "as you continue to play," in the definition of Mathematical Expectation. Another paradox emerges: How much of a cover charge, if any, is a fair price for entering such a game, given the potential heat you may endure, the certain profit you will see, and the time it may take for that profit to manifest?

[2]Though the Leverage Space Model is presented as specifying risk as drawdown rather than variance in returns or some other ersatz measure of risk, it is feasible to incorporate these other risk measures, either in tandem with drawdown, or in solitary fashion, using the Leverage Space Model. For example, if a manager is indexed to a variance-based benchmark, such as the Sharpe Ratio, he *could* employ the Leverage Space Model, paring away those points on the terrain where either the drawdown constraint *or* his variance constraint was violated, thus making points that violate either constraint be unacceptable portfolio combinations.

[3]Recall in the Leverage Space Model that if one is trading in a constant-unit size (as opposed to trading in size relative to equity), one is migrating toward the $f_1 \ldots f_n = 0_1 \ldots 0_n$ point in leverage space as the equity increases and, similarly, toward the $f_1 \ldots f_n = 1_1 \ldots 1_n$ point in leverage space as the equity decreases. Since we are always within the terrain of leverage space, whether we acknowledge it or not, the approach presented, for instance, a Martingale-style approach, can be said to be an approach that seeks a path through the terrain of leverage space itself. Hence, we see firsthand here how the Leverage Space Model is not merely a static model of allocation, but a paradigm for more dynamic-types of allocations as well.

probability of being at or above a given return by a specific future point, within the constraint of not exceeding a given probability of touching or exceeding a lower absorbing barrier through the duration toward that future point. This lower barrier may be fixed (for instance, "ruin") or allowed to float upwards as a percentage of equity increase (for instance, "drawdown").

Serendipitously, a small Martingale-type approach is consistent with the preferred investor behavior regarding risk aversion posited in "Prospect Theory," and as such, ought to be psychologically easier for an investor or fund manager to implement.

In brief, Prospect Theory asserts that humans have a greater tendency to gamble more under accrued losses (for instance, a small Martingale) in an attempt to maximize the probability of profit at a future point in time, whereas those confronted with profits seem to be more risk-averse,[4] save the rare, freelance madman who truly *is* a profit maximizer.

Given the propensity of humans to maximize the probability of profit at a given horizon in time, it is the fund manager's responsibility and preference to pursue that within a given drawdown constraint. In one of those rare conjugal visits of mathematics and human behavior, we seek here to identify that function for probability of profit maximization versus risk, as both a tool for the portfolio manager as well as the mathematical operating function of human behavior under conditions of risk.

ALGORITHM AND FORMULAS

If we have a variable (a "Martingale exponent") denoted as z greater than -1 and less than or equal to zero, then:

$$-1 < z <= 0 \tag{7.01}$$

We can then say that

$$1/(1 + z) - 1 \tag{7.02}$$

gives a result from 0 to infinity, as Table 7.1 demonstrates.

Note that since we are going to be trading a small Martingale, we are not trading a fraction of our stake, so there is seemingly no f value for the components and hence no $f\$$ value.

---

[4]The pervasiveness of this tendency in humans and other primates (Chen et al. 2006) is suggestive of an evolutionary cause, a hard wiring of a given function.

TABLE 7.1	Trading a Small Martingale; There Is Seemingly No f Value for the Components and Hence No $f\$$ Value

$-z$	$1/(1 + z) - 1$
Approach -1	Approach Infinity
from the right	from the left
-0.9999	10000
-0.999	1000
-0.9901	100
-0.98039	50
-0.97087	33.33333
-0.96154	25
-0.95238	20
-0.9434	16.66667
-0.8	4
-0.66667	2
-0.5	1
-0.37879	0.609756
-0.04762	0.05
-0.0099	0.01
0	0

However, we do need a context, an initial capitalization of a component, a scenario spectrum, and we will retain a consistent nomenclature and call this initial capitalization the component's $f\$$ (that is, the amount we divide the current total capital of an account by to know how many "units" to put on for the current position).

Because we have an $f\$$ for each component, and a scenario comprising the largest losing outcome for each component, we can discern an "initial f" value for each component (as that value wherein the absolute value of the outcome result of the biggest losing scenario divided by equals the $f\$$).

$$|\text{Biggest Losing Outcome}|/f = f\$ \qquad (1.09)$$

Thus:

$$|\text{Biggest Losing Outcome}|/f\$ = f \qquad (2.01)$$

Suppose we currently have \$120,000 in equity. Further suppose we have on 300 shares of a given stock, and we determine that one unit is 100 shares. We thus have three units on currently—so we can say that our current $f\$$ is \$40,000, representing the amount we are capitalizing a unit by. Lastly, suppose we know our largest losing scenario assigned to a unit of this stock is \$10,000 (per unit, that is, per 100 shares). Now we can determine *our de facto f* value as (always $0 >= f <= 1$):

$$|-10,000|/40,000 = .25$$

In a Leverage Space Model–style portfolio, regardless of the individual components, when the portfolio is up, more quantity is traded and vice versa. Similarly now, but in reverse, we will trade more quantity on the downside for all components, while retaining their ratios to each other. This is the notion of *diversifying risk*, whereby stronger elements at the time support the weaker ones.

The process now proceeds as follows. At each holding period (i, of q holding periods), for each component (k, of N components), we adjust the $f\$$ for the component that period as follows:

$$f\$_{k,i} = \frac{BL_k/-f_k}{\left(\dfrac{acctEQ_0}{acctEQ_{i-1}}\right)^{\left(\frac{1}{(1+z)}-1\right)}} \tag{7.03}$$

where: $f\$_{k,i} =$ the amount to allocate to the kth component on the ith holding period
$BL_k =$ the largest losing scenario outcome for the kth component, a negative number
$f_k =$ the initial f value ($0 <= f <= 1$) for the kth component, based on its initial capitalization
$acctEQ_0 =$ the account equity before the first holding period (that is, the initial equity)
$acctEQ_{i-1} =$ the account equity immediately before the current period
$z =$ the "Martingale exponent," value from (7.01)

Note that the $f\$_{k,i}$ returned can be converted into a current f_k, which then is the point where our path for $acctEQ_0/acctEQ_{i-1}$. This function therefore gives our path through leverage space to maximize the probability of profit. *This then is our migration function.* It is one means, one type of migration function, that can be implemented to maximize for highest probability of profit at some horizon.

We will employ two separate z values, so that our function is consistent with that of Prospect Theory, which demonstrated empirically people's

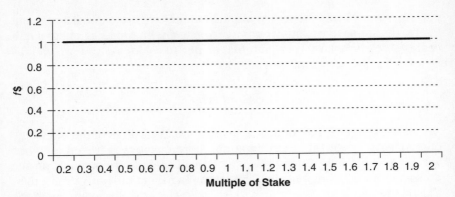

FIGURE 7.1 $z_- = 0$, $z_+ = 0$

different risk preferences when they were "up" from a given reference point as opposed to "down" from the given reference point.

Thus, we have one z value for when our stake is down from its starting value (that is, a multiple on the starting stake <1) and a different z value when the multiple on the starting stake >1. We will call these values z_- and z_+ respectively.

Note that in (7.03) at $z = 0$ the investor's capitalization per unit remains constant (hence the investor is still trading less as his equity is diminishing). We can show these relationships graphically, and we will assume our initial $f\$$ (when multiple = 1) is \$1. This is shown in Figure 7.1.

Thus, Figure 7.1 demonstrates that regardless of equity, at $z = 0$ the number of units put on will always be the current equity divided by the same initial $f\$$ amount. As the account equity diminishes, so, too, will the units put on, and vice versa.

At $z = -.5$ the capitalization is such that the number of units the investor trades in is constant. Thus, at $z = -.5$, the number of units he trades will always be the same regardless of account equity. This is demonstrated in Figure 7.2.

When $z < -.5$, the investor begins to capitalize units with ever-less amounts, thus incurring a Martingale-type effect. Again, since preferences among human beings seem to be a function of whether one is up or down from a given reference point (that is, where multiple = 1), we allow two separate z values to accommodate this very human propensity, though, as the previous two figures demonstrated, these two values could be set equal to each other.

Figure 7.3 shows (7.03) in a typical, real-life example of two separate z values.

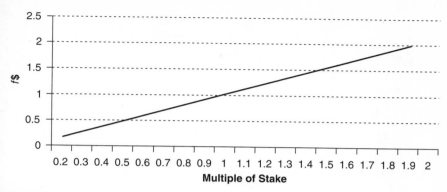

FIGURE 7.2 $z_- = -.5$, $z_+ = -.5$

Figure 7.3 begins to accomplish the small Martingale effect, innate in Prospect Theory, which seeks to maximize profits at a given future point. Table 7.2 shows Figure 7.3 in tabular form.

It is my contention that (7.03) is the evolutionary hard-wired function in humans pertaining to risk seeking and risk aversion, and is consistent in graphical form with what has been posited by Prospect Theory.

Since (7.03) is the evolutionary-wired preference in humans, a fund manager's "success" becomes a function of the degree to which he satisfies this preference in his clients.

Note that in a straight Martingale progression (betting 1, 2, 4, 8, 16, *ad infinitum* after a loss until a win is seen), it is only after a winning play that the account value is up. In all other situations, the account is actually down most of the time, often quite substantially if during a run of losing plays. Thus, a straight Martingale can be said to put an account up at some

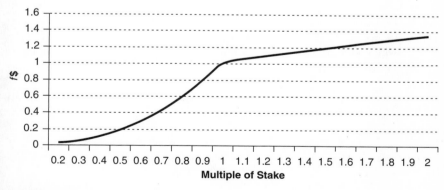

FIGURE 7.3 $z_- = -.7$, $z_+ - .3$

TABLE 7.2	Figure 7.3 Shown In Tabular Form
Multiple E	**f%**
0.1	0.004641589
0.2	0.023392142
0.3	0.060248966
0.4	0.117889008
0.5	0.198425131
0.6	0.30363576
0.7	0.435072961
0.8	0.594123371
0.9	0.782046402
1	1
1.1	1.041692943
1.2	1.081271659
1.3	1.11900716
1.4	1.155117866
1.5	1.189782789
1.6	1.223150769
1.7	1.255347099
1.8	1.28647841
1.9	1.316636313
2	1.345900193

arbitrary point in the future, but not necessarily at some *given* point in the future.

That's why the function (7.03) "breaks" at a multiple $= 1$, by virtue of having two separate Martingale exponents (z_- and z_+). Note that when an account is up, the bet size diminishes as a function of both the multiple on the starting stake, and the Martingale exponent z_+. This part of the formula, consistent with the empirically observed behavior of Prospect Theory, permits a small Martingale progression the opportunity to retain profits efficiently until the horizon, the *given* future point (as opposed to the *arbitrary* one), is seen.

In (7.03), since $f\$_{k,i}$ = the amount to allocate to the kth component on the ith holding period, we can determine the number of units to trade for the kth component on the ith holding period as:

$$U_{k,i} = \frac{acctEQ_{i-1}}{f\$_{k,i}} \qquad (7.04)$$

or, since $f\$_{k,i}$ is given by equation (7.03):

$$U_{k,i} = \frac{\frac{acctEQ_{i-1}}{BL_k/-f_k}}{\left(\frac{acctEQ_0}{acctEQ_{i-1}}\right)^{\left(\frac{1}{(1+z)}-1\right)}} \qquad (7.04a)$$

Dividing current equity by the $f\$$ given in (7.03) for each component tells us how many units to have on for each component $(1 \ldots N)$ at each holding period $(1 \ldots q)$.

We will now attempt to find the Martingale exponents $(z_-$ and $z_+)$ for the portfolio, and the set of initial $f_{1 \ldots N}$ for its components that maximize the probability of profit (PP), at some given horizon. We can also discern this with respect to a given probability of a given drawdown or risk of ruin, at that horizon point, per the technique given in Chapter 5, with slight amendments provided at the end of this chapter.

Note that you trade more units when the account is down, and less when it is up. The Martingale exponents $(z_-$ and $z_+)$ are the levers that govern this. We will then seek those values for the Martingale exponents $(z_-$ and $z_+)$ for the portfolio, and the set of initial $f_{1 \ldots N}$ for its components so as to maximize the probability of profit, $PP(r)$, at some given horizon, where r typically is 0. If, for example, we considered "profit," as a 2 percent return at the horizon, we would say that we seek to maximize $PP(.02)$.

Note we can still calculate our TWR$(f_1 \ldots f_N)$ (Terminal Wealth Relative) as:

$$TWR(f_1 \ldots f_N) = \frac{acctEQ_q}{acctEQ_0} \qquad (7.05)$$

since TWR$(f_1 \ldots f_N)$ is simply the multiple we have made on our stake, after q holding periods.

Note a different scenario occurs at each holding period. We wish to maximize the probability of profit, $PP(r)$, for a given r (our minimum return, which, if exceeded, we consider being "profitable"), over a given number of holding periods, q.

For the sake of simplicity, assume a coin toss, wherein one of two possible scenarios, heads or tails (H or T), can occur. If we decide to look at $q = 2$ holding periods, there are four possible branches that can be traversed, as follows:

H	H
H	T
T	H
T	T

Note that in this case of two possible scenarios ($q = 2$ holding periods) there are four possible branches of traversal. This is the process detailed in Chapter 5 for branch traversal in determining drawdown probabilities.

Similarly, if we assume a portfolio of two coins, each with the same possible two scenarios of heads and tails, we see:

HH	HH
HH	HT
HH	TH
HH	TT
HT	HH
HT	HT
HT	TH
HT	TT
TH	HH
TH	HT
TH	TH
TH	TT
TT	HH
TT	HT
TT	TH
TT	TT

Each branch sees its own TWR($f_1 \ldots f_N$) calculation from (7.05). Thus, for each branch, we can determine whether

$$TWR(f_1 \ldots f_N) - 1 \geq r \qquad (7.06)$$

for that branch, and if so, we conclude that the branch is "profitable." Thus, since we want to optimize for highest probability of profit, we therefore want to maximize the ratio of the number of branches satisfying (7.06) divided by the total number of branches—this represents the Probability of Profit function, $PP(r)$, which is what we seek to maximize by altering the Martingale exponents (z_- and z_+) for the portfolio, and the set of initial $f_{1\ldots N}$ for its components.

The process for doing this, that is, finishing at or above an upper absorbing barrier (at time q), is very similar to the process of determining drawdown—that is, touching or exceeding a lower absorbing barrier (at any time $0 \ldots q$).

We use the branching process described in Chapter 5 to determine this, yet in determining the probability of profit we are concerned only if the *terminal* leaves on the branching process are at or above r, unlike drawdown, where we are concerned whether, at *any point* along the branch, b (Chapter 5 as $RX(b)$) has been touched on the downside. Thus, at each terminal node in the branch, we assess (7.06).

The calculation to determine the $acctEQ_y$ at any point $(y = 1 \dots q)$ is given as:

$$acctEQ_y = \sum_{i=1}^{y} \sum_{k=1}^{N} (U_{k,i} * outcome_{k,i}) \qquad (7.07)$$

or

$$acctEQ_y = \sum_{i=1}^{y} \sum_{k=1}^{N} \left(\left(\frac{acctEQ_{i-1}}{f\$_{k,i}} \right) * outcome_{k,i} \right) \qquad (7.07a)$$

where: $outcome_{k,i} =$ the kth component's scenario outcome at point i in the branching process
$f\$_{k,i} =$ given by equation (7.03)

Now we can look at the values at the terminal leaf of each branch, and assess (7.06). Each branch has a probability associated with it. By taking the sum of these probabilities as our denominator, and the sum of the probabilities for those branches that satisfy (7.06) as our numerator, we derive a $PP(r)$ for a given set of Martingale exponents (z_- and z_+) and set of initial $f_{1 \dots N}$ values that we are optimizing over to determine greatest $PP(r)$ within an (optional) drawdown/risk of ruin constraint.

Since the process of maximizing probability of profit is an additive one (as opposed to maximizing for profit, which is a multiplicative one), we must amend our calculation for β *in* Chapter 5 (5.03). If we are determining risk of ruin, we then have $RR(b)$,

$$\text{int} \left(\frac{\sum_{i=1}^{q} acctEQ_i / acctEQ_0 - b}{\sum_{i=1}^{q} |(acctEQ_i / acctEQ_0 - b)|} \right) = \beta \qquad (5.03')$$

supplanting (5.03).

Given the propinquity of drawdown and ruin, we must adjust for the case of *Risk of Drawdown*, $RD(b)$, and supplanting (5.03a) we have:

$$\text{int} \left(\frac{\sum_{i=1}^{q} (acctEQ_i / \max(acctEQ_0 \cdots acctEQ_i) - b)}{\sum_{i=1}^{q} |(acctEQ_i / \max(acctEQ_0 \cdots acctEQ_i) - b)|} \right) = \beta \qquad (5.03a')$$

Supplanting (5.03a).

Note that we can perform the calculation for both $PP(r)$ and $RX(b)$ simultaneously in the branching process per the algorithm provided in Chapter 5. However, it must be pointed out that if the lower absorbing barrier, b, is seen while traversing a branch, the branch must still be fully traversed to determine (7.06). That is, simply hitting a drawdown on the branch does not permit one to abort the branch altogether—the branch must still be fully traversed so as not to sabotage the probability of profit calculation.

The altitude is the altitude in the sense mentioned throughout, but the *real* altitude for a migration function is where the investor finishes after q trials, and may be above or below the surface of the leverage space.

Let's return to the St. Petersburg Paradox. Where is our altitude after, say, five trials?

$$ME = 2^0 * \frac{1}{2^1} + 2^1 * \frac{1}{2^2} + 2^2 * \frac{1}{2^3} + 2^3 * \frac{1}{2^4} + 2^4 * \frac{1}{2^5} \qquad (1.01)$$

$$ME = 1 * \frac{1}{2} + 2 * \frac{1}{4} + 4 * \frac{1}{8} + 8 * \frac{1}{16} + 16 * \frac{1}{32}$$

$$ME = 1 * .5 + 2 * .25 + 4 * .125 + 8 * .0625 + 16 * .03125$$

$$ME = .5 + .5 + .5 + .5 + .5$$

$$ME = 2.5$$

By determining our Mathematical Expectation, at q plays, divided by our starting stake, we can determine our TWR per equation (7.05).

The question posed by the St. Petersburg Paradox, which asks what a "fair" cover charge would be, is, in fact, the paradox. If the game ends after five plays, rather than continuing on indefinitely, a fair cover charge would then be the Mathematical Expectation at $q = 5$, which, as we see, is 2.5.

However, for argument's sake, let's assume the cover charge was two units. Then, per (7.05):

$$TWR = 2.5/2 = 1.25$$

This, then, is our altitude in the $N+1$–dimensional landscape after q trials, as given by (7.05).

In short, we determine what we would expect to make at q, divided by the starting stake. This gives us our TWR (or, the qth root, giving the GHPR) that *is* the altitude in the $N+1$–dimensional landscape.

With regard to maximizing the probability of being profitable, how can we determine, for this migration function, what we would expect to make at q?

For the answer, let's go back to our real-world example, as determined from Chapter 4:

MktSysA	MktSysB	MktSysC	Probability	Scenario#
−$150.00	$253.00	$533.00	0.076923077	1
−$45.33	−$1,000.00	$220.14	0.076923077	2
−$45.33	−$64.43	$220.14	0.153846154	3
$13.00	−$64.43	−$500.00	0.076923077	4
$13.00	−$64.43	$533.00	0.076923077	5
$13.00	$253.00	$220.14	0.076923077	6
$13.00	$253.00	$799.00	0.076923077	7
$13.00	$448.00	$220.14	0.076923077	8
$79.67	−$64.43	−$325.00	0.076923077	9
$79.67	−$64.43	$220.14	0.076923077	10
$79.67	−$64.43	$533.00	0.076923077	11
$136.00	$253.00	$220.14	0.076923077	12

We want to determine the expected value at horizontal node q. Thus, at the first horizontal node ($y = 1$, en route to 12), we have 12 scenario outcomes, and these branch each time y is incremented, as we have done repeatedly throughout the text.

Ultimately, we end up at horizontal point (time) q, and thus have 12^q nodes. Each node has a probability to it, which is the product of the scenario probabilities at each y.

For example, if we have $q = 3$, we have $12^3=1,728$ terminal nodes. Each node has a probability associated with it, which is the product of the probabilities to that node at each y. We will then have scenarios 1-1-1 as a terminal node,1-1-2...12-12-12. One of those 1,728 terminal nodes will be 8-3-11, which would then see a probability for that terminal node of $0.076923077 * 0.153846154 * 0.076923077 = 0.000910332$.

Also, each terminal node has an outcome, as determined by equation (7.07). To determine the outcome (7.07) at point q for a given branch, it must be determined for all subsequent branches to q, starting at 1.

When I have all 1,728 branches' outcomes and their associated probabilities at q, I can multiply the outcomes by the probabilities and take the sum of these 1,728 products (this is simply Mathematical Expectation). Dividing this by my starting equity (equity at $q = 0$) gives me my TWR(f_1, f_2, f_3) (with given z_-, z_+). This is my altitude in the $N+1$–dimensional landscape of leverage space (four-dimensional in this case), and is *above* the surface. Of course, to the qth root of this TWR(f_1, f_2, f_3) is my GHPR(f_1, f_2, f_3) (with given z_-, z_+).

For a single 2:1 coin toss, maximizing for highest probability of profit at five periods out, within a drawdown constraint of not more than a 10 percent chance of a 20 percent drawdown, we can discern numerous parameter values that result in the same probability of profit of .96875. One of these has the following parameters:

$$f = 0.041 \text{ and thus } f\$ = 24.41$$
$$z_- = -0.848$$
$$z_+ = -0.996$$
$$RD(0.8, 0.1, 5) = 0.0625$$

Yes, the probability of a drawdown of 20 percent within the first five plays at these parameter values is .0625, a 6.25 percent probability, well under our 10 percent constraint.

Returning to how much we would expect to make (our mathematical expectation) after five plays, we need to begin the branching process. Let us assume we start with $f\$$ in our stake of 24.41 and that units are infinitely divisible (we could start with a much larger number in our initial stake, say, 1,000,000,000 units and say that units are *not* divisible to achieve the same ends).

Thus, at $q = 0$ our stake $= 24.41$. At $q = 1$, we have two branches, one with heads, one with tails, and they continue to branch to $q = 5$.

```
                                                                h       h
                                                    h                   t
                                                    t           t       h
                                        h                               t
                                                    h           h       h
                                        t                       t
                            h                       t           t       h
                                        h                               t
                                        h           h           h       h
                                                                t
                            t           t           t           h       t
                                        t                               h
                                                    h           h       t
                                        t                       t
                                                    t           t       h
start                                                           h       t
                                                    h                   h
                                        h                       h       t
                                                    t                   h
                                                                t       t
                                                                        h
```

```
                    h                                           t
                                            h                   h
                            t                                   t
                                            t                   h
            t                                                   t
                                            h                   h
                            h                                   t
                                            t                   h
            t                                                   t
                                            h                   h
                            t                                   t
                                            t                   h
                                                                t

q=0         1           2           3           4           5
```

With an $f\$$ value of 24.14 and $z_- = -0.848$ and $z_+ = -0.996$, we can traverse the branches of this tree, solving for equation (7.07) at each node, obtaining:

```
                                                            26.4
                                                26.4        26.4
                                    26.4                    26.4
                                                26.4        26.4
                        26.4                                26.4
                                                26.4        26.4
                                    26.4                    26.4
                                                26.4        26.4
            26.4                                            26.4
                                                26.4        26.4
                                    26.4                    26.4
                                                26.4        26.4
                        26.4                                26.4
                                                26.4        26.4
                                    26.4                    26.4
                                                26.4        26.4
  start                                                     25.8
                                                25.8        25.8
                                    25.8                    25.8
                                                25.8        25.8
                        25.8                                25.8
                                                25.8        25.8
                                    25.8                    25.8
```

$q=0$	1	2	3	4	5
				25.8	25.8
	23.4				25.3
				25.3	25.3
			25.3		25.3
				25.3	25.3
		22.2			25
				25	24.9
			20.7		25.6
				18.5	15

Note that of the 32 terminal leaves, 31 of them were profitable at $q = 5$ (13/32 = .96875). Further, note that 2 of the branches saw a 20 percent or greater drawdown between $q = 1$ and $q = 5$ inclusively (2/32 = .0625).

I chose a single coin toss with $q = 5$, $n = 2$ in this example, because the numbers are manageable and provide an example presentable here to convey the algorithmic exercise in determining the expected altitude in the $N+2$–dimensional landscape (2D in this case) at $q = 5$.

It should be noted that you would be migrating about at different values for f from $q = 2$ through $q = 5$, but at $q = 5$ your expected altitude is the TWR(.041), or the sum of the terminal leaves, divided by the number of terminal leaves (25.65138409) divided by the starting equity (24.41). Thus 25.65138409 / 24.41 = 1.050855555. This is my altitude in the $N+1$–dimensional (2D in this case) landscape at $q = 5$. Thus, I can figure my GHPR(.041) by taking this to the 5th root ($1.050855555^{1/5} = 1.001551347$).

Again, the computational aspect is considerable as q and n get larger! Shortcut methods such as those presented in the previous chapters should be employed where possible to obtain good approximations.

But where are you, really, on this surface at $q = 5$? Ultimately, that's a function of the particular terminal leaf you are at. In our example, f for the first 31 leaves at $q = 5$ is nearly 0, and for the last leaf it is .631156 (because we take the terminal leaf value of 14.15924 and via equation (7.05a) we determine our number of units to wager on the next play as 1.58439423, whereas, if the absolute value of our biggest loss ($|-1| = 1$) is divided by this value (1 /1.58439423 = .631156) per equation (2.01), we determine this is an f coordinate of .631156 for the 32nd branch of this tree, going into $q = 6$.

The real-time implementation of a migration path is a straightforward affair, once the f values z_+ and z_- are determined within the given horizon (q) and drawdown parameters.

Implementation is straightforward and not complicated. Some may argue that the mathematics behind the Leverage Space framework are complicated, but the implementation is nevertheless easy. With a grasp of the conceptual underpinnings of leverage space, sans math, you can perceive what you are working within. With a viable migration function, created to achieve your goals, implementation becomes merely a matter of implementing the migration function on a real-time basis.

Returning again to our three-market example from the previous chapters, if we seek the highest probability of profit, with $q = 12$ (that is, over the course of the next 12 months) within a 10 percent probability of no more than a 20 percent drawdown, we find our probability of profit is almost 100 percent, and the probability of such a drawdown is .012, utilizing the following parameters:

	f	$f\$$
MktSysA	0.085	$1,762.19
MktSysB	0.015	$67,956.90
MktSysC	0.129	$3,879.44
$z_- =$	−0.76	
$z_+ =$	−0.992	

We can set up a spreadsheet to implement a migration path quite easily. Once we have determined our initial f and z values, which maximize the probability of profit at a given horizon (q), we have all the input we need to perform the real-time implementation. To begin with, we need to input our starting and current equity, as well as the two z values. This appears in the first four rows.

We also need, for each market system, the initial f, biggest loss and worst-case outcome. This is seen beginning at row 8, and columns A through D.

	A	B	C	D	E
1	Starting Equity		$1,000,000.00		
2	Current Equity		$1,000,000.00		
3	z_+		−0.992		
4	z_-		−0.76		
5					
6					
7		Initial f	Worst Case	Current $f\$$	Units
8	MktSysA	0.085	−$150.00	$1,764.71	566
9	MktSysB	0.015	−$1,000.00	$66,666.67	15
10	MktSysC	0.129	−$500.00	$3,875.97	258

The current $f\$$ requires formulation. Essentially, for cell D8, in Microsoft Excel, we input the formula:

$$= \text{IF}(\$C\$2 > \$C\$1, (C8/-B8)/((\$C\$1/\$C\$2)^\wedge((1/(1+\$C\$3))-1)),$$
$$\text{IF}(\$C\$2 < \$C\$1, (C8/-B8)/((\$C\$1/\$C\$2)^\wedge((1/(1+\$C\$4))-1)),$$
$$C8/-B8))$$

We then copy down this cell to the remainder rows in column D.

Lastly, column E is calculated, starting with cell E8 as:

$$= INT(\$C\$2/D8)$$

We then copy down this cell to the remainder rows in column E.

At the end of each holding period (one month in our example case), we need only change the current equity, cell C2. We will then have, in column E, the corresponding correct number of units that we should have on for each market system, so as to be consistent with what our research showed, with the scenarios and their joint probabilities working out to provide for the maximum probability of profit.

Thus, we would adjust our current positions to reflect the new "units" column, column E, at the end of each holding period.

Debate continues as to how frequently one can best "readjust" to what is shown as the quantity an investor should have on. There is no clean, simple answer that I am aware of. It is a function of transaction costs, liquidity, the length of the holding period, the types of market systems (not all are in the market all of the time), futures and options contract rollovers, and so on.

Consider an individual day trader who makes multiple trades daily, all in one market system ($N = 1$). His holding period may ideally be one trade (rather than a period of time, which is what one should use when $N > 1$). He can thus reallocate with each trade optimally, if the data that he puts into the spreadsheet is discerned from a scenario spectrum that was constructed using individual trades.

Let's continue with our three-market system example. We'll assume, since we are using months as holding periods, that the first month has elapsed, and we witness something along the lines of scenario #4 of these three-market systems. That is, the one-unit outcomes for each market system are $13.00, -$64.43, -$500 respectively. This would be a net loss for the first month, at the prescribed quantities of $122,608.45, leaving the account value at $877,391.55.

The only thing we need to do is to put this value into cell C2 to obtain what our new quantities should be, and adjust them in the marketplace accordingly:

	A	B	C	D	E
1	Starting Equity		$1,000,000.00		
2	Current Equity		$877,391.55		
3	z_+		−0.992		
4	z_-		−0.76		
5					
6					
7		Initial f	Worst Case	Current $f\$$	Units
8	MktSysA	0.085	−$150.00	$1,166.23	752
9	MktSysB	0.015	−$1,000.00	$44,057.65	19
10	MktSysC	0.129	−$500.00	$2,561.49	342

Now suppose that for the next month we see the manifestation of scenario #7 as gains of $13, $253, and $799 respectively for MktSysA, MktSysB, and MktSysC. This results in a net gain for the month of $287,841.00, putting the current equity at the end of the month at $1,165,232.55. Again, we update our current equity:

	A	B	C	D	E
1	Starting Equity		$1,000,000.00		
2	Current Equity		$1,165,232.55		
3	z_+		−0.992		
4	z_-		−0.76		
5					
6					
7		Initial f	Worst Case	Current $f\$$	Units
8	MktSysA	0.085	−$150.00	$300 billion+	0
9	MktSysB	0.015	−$1,000.00	$11 trillion+	0
10	MktSysC	0.129	−$500.00	$666 billion+	0

Notice what happens to our number of units. We have effectively stopped trading with a profit. This is due to our z_+ value of −.992.

In the real world, you can set constraints at the lowest you will allow a z_- or z_+ value to go. For example, you may opt to not allow z_- to get below −.75, and not allow z_+ to get below −.8. Such a procedure would keep you from shutting down entirely on the upside, or taking on potentially enormous quantities after protracted drawdowns.

Once the horizon is reached (that is, once $q = 12$), 12 months will have elapsed in our example, we set the starting equity to the current equity, and we begin the process anew.

PROBABILITY OF PROFIT AS A CONSTRAINT IN MAXIMIZING PROFIT

Often our concern is *not only* a matter of maximizing for the greatest probability of profit within a given drawdown constraint. There is also the *secondary* concern of maximizing profit. Therefore, rather than maximizing for the greatest probability of profit, one can maximize for the greatest profit, within a given minimal probability of profit (profit $>= r$) and within a given drawdown constraint.

As a result, the probability of profit becomes a constraint, just as probability of drawdown is a constraint. The criterion now, it would seem, is to once again maximize gains.

You would think, then, that those points on the leverage space terrain, where the probability of profit to a certain horizon was not within prescribed parameters, would result in holes in that landscape in the same way that exceeding prescribed drawdown parameters affects coordinates on the landscape.

That, however, is *not* the case.

Again, because we are employing equation (7.03) to find the optimal z_- and z_+, we are migrating about the landscape of leverage space. Furthermore, the terrain of leverage space, ripped by the coordinates where drawdown exceeds the prescribed parameters, is altered by formulaic changes required in seeking the highest $PP(r)$ from equations (5.03') and (5.03a').

So, if we want to maximize *profit*, within a given drawdown constraint, and within a given probability of profit, our changes are simply algorithmic ones. Again, we are looking for that path through leverage space—the effect of the drawdown constraint, altered by (5.03') or (5.03a')—given by the values z_- and z_+, that sees the greatest altitude at the horizon, q, provided the $PP(r)$ constraint is not violated at q.

Once again, what we expect to make, on average, at q, as a multiple on our stake, is a function of the migration function and must be determined for a given migration function, as has been demonstrated in this chapter. It is not the altitude of a coordinate set on the surface in leverage space—rather, it is calculated by taking the value of the stake, at each terminal leaves, times the probability of that leaf, and summing this product of the leafs together, divided by the number of terminal leaves. This quotient is then the numerator, with the starting stake as the denominator, thus obtaining the TWR. The determination of the value at each terminal leaf is a function of the migration function itself.

This results in a different path through leverage space (that is, different values for z_- and z_+) than merely maximizing for highest $PP(r)$. Typically, this will provide a slightly greater z_+ value (that is, closer to 0, from below, than you would get for simply maximizing for greatest probability of profit, the latter having you typically stop trading nearly altogether, if not altogether, once a profit is achieved at $< q$ elapsed periods).

However, the real-time implementation is exactly as was demonstrated for the case of optimizing simply for greatest probability of profit. Your z_+ and z_- can be plugged into a spreadsheet, along with your starting equity, current equity, and initial f values to determine how many contracts to presently have on for each market system.

The result is one that satisfies many of the demands on money managers. However, the demands on you may be different. These examples (though they do satisfy many) provide you with the tools and show you the implementation to achieve precisely the criteria that you want.

FORMULA PLANS

Beginning in the 1940s, one can find a cornucopia of mostly now long-lost ideas that were referred to at the time as "formula plans."[5] These were formulaic methods that were advocated for entering, adding to, and lightening up on exiting positions. Something like dollar cost averaging can be considered a simple and age-old example of what would constitute a formula plan. Similarly, with more modern notions such as "Portfolio Insurance" or the notion of "Continuous Dominance," presented in (Vince 1995, 2007).

Formula Plans were a huge fad in the 1940s and 1950s. However, the then-nascent concept of Modern Portfolio Theory pushed these ideas into seeming extinction, and by the 1970s, most of these ideas seemed to have become dinosaurs.

Though not referred to as formula plans, many market practitioners today are employing what could be called a formula plan. For example, the notion of adjusting one's quantity for a forthcoming trade as a function of a market's current volatility is, in essence, a formula plan.

Unfortunately for the proponents of formula plans in the middle twentieth century, they didn't have the Leverage Space Model—they didn't have the mathematical framework to really see what they were doing. However, they knew that by employing these plans, they could produce returns, restrict losses, and deal with market conditions to points they could live with.

Yet a formula plan is, in effect, a migration path! There is perhaps fecund territory to resurrect some of these ideas in the context of Leverage Space, of re-distillation into formulaic migration paths. In the past, such

---

[5]I am indebted to John Bollinger for having pointed out to me the formula plan concepts and their relation to the notion of migration functions.

plans sought to achieve certain criteria. Now, these ideas have a context they can be placed in, one that is congruent with the notion of migrating about a space of available portfolio allocations such as we have been discussing.

APPLICATION TO NEGATIVE EXPECTATIONS

The approaches presented in this chapter—the migration functions for maximizing the probability of profit, or maximizing profit within a given probability of profit constraint—are applicable to and beneficial in helping weather negative expectation games as well as periods where things don't quite go as planned, that is, when the distributions of returns experienced diverge from the scenario spectrums used as input. Arguably, one of the unexpected benefits of managing a portfolio, of adjusting quantity based on migration functions that are consistent with Prospect Theory, is that they *do* very efficiently absorb the effects of negative expectations as well as the negative expectation that often manifests of things not going according to plan.

First, you'll recall from the Introduction to this text the lottery mentioned with a negative expectation (a lottery wherein you are given $1 every week, with a one-in-one-million chance of losing $2 million dollars, the Mathematical Expectation being therefore −1.000001 per week).

It was pointed out that this was not necessarily a bad bet. In the overwhelming majority of 50-year spans (roughly 399 out of 400), you would expect to collect $2,600. Life is finite; the amount of plays you will get is finite; the number of holding periods you will encounter is necessarily finite. Thus, negative expectation is not necessarily the kiss of death.

Provided one can budget for the worst-case scenario, Mathematical Expectation is not necessarily a good criterion for assessing a risk unless the horizon you intend to participate in gives that expectation the opportunity to manifest. Clearly, if we were to play for one million weeks, we could assume we would, on average, lose $2 million against a gain of $999,999 from the remaining weeks where we won $1. The parameters of this game are different, than, say, a game with a .4999995 probability of winning $1,000,001 and a .5000005 probability of losing $1,000,001 (giving us the same Mathematical Expectation of −1.000001 per week).

Mathematical Expectation is a crude tool. It has an element of information loss to it that is crucial in assessing risks, the element of time for its manifestation to materialize on average. Just as was pointed out in Chapter 4, correlation/covariance/beta are crude tools for assessing intermarket relationships, so too is Mathematical Expectation a crude tool for assessing risk prospects.

The second and more important point to consider about negative expectation games (including the temporary case of negative expectation—those cases where things don't go as planned) pertains to the (small) Martingale progression allowing us to overcome the negative expectation by virtue of the point just mentioned and a small initial unit size.

Reconsider Table 5.1, and specifically row 8, where we now see a dramatic increase in our probabilities of success. As pointed out by (Epstein 1967, p. 60), *"With large initial capital, there is a high probability of winning a small amount even in games that are slightly unfavorable."*

Any type of Martingale progression (large or small) will necessarily have you starting out risking smaller quantities, in order to execute the (small) Martingale progression, if necessary.

Thus, an initial outlay consistent with being able to execute the progression to the extent you have budgeted for is paramount in order to execute a small Martingale. The probabilities of being able to weather and turn profitable a nearly unrealistic string of losses can be budgeted for by making the initial wager size be extremely small relative to the total stake.

For instance, assume a standard Martingale where we double the stake on every play, in a game with a .5 probability of winning 1 unit, and a .5 probability of losing 1 unit (for simplicity). Now, we assume 20 losers in a row, the probabilities of which are $1 / 2^{20} = 1/1,048,576 = .000000954$. Note: We need 1,048,576 for the twenty-first (2^{20}) wager. Thus, if we play this game, whereby our stake is large enough and our initial wager is small enough such that our initial wager in this full-Martingale game is $1 / 2,097,151^{th}$ of our stake, we will have budgeted for the extreme probability of seeing 20 consecutive losing plays, budgeted for something that has a .000000954 probability of occurrence, and thus insured a very high probability of winning a small amount in this even-money game (the situation is similar if we make the game negative—the parameters presented are done so for simplicity of illustration).

On the upside, note how we wager less and less, depending upon the z_+ exponent (we may even be required to stop wagering altogether in this negative expectation run, wherein we are now at a net gain).

To be clear, *having the option of quitting after each play does not affect Mathematical Expectation.* (John Venn, the British philosopher and logician known for his contributions to Set Theory, successfully showed that an advantage *does* accrue to a player who has the option of quitting after each play, provided he has infinite wealth. However, it has been subsequently demonstrated that finite wealth does, in fact, alter this conclusion.)

Yet, we aren't stopping play, or utilizing our z_+ Martingale exponent to affect Mathematical Expectation. Rather, we are using it as an opportunity to sit out the balance of a negative expectation to our horizon, should we encounter the good fortune of being profitable at some point.

Our Prospect Theory based implementation of a small Martingale is not a misguided attempt to turn a negative expectation game into a positive one, to weather a period where things don't go as planned. Rather, it provides us far greater opportunities to come through to our horizons with a profit than most other approaches. In short, an approach such as the one presented, versus other types of approaches, helps us come out of periods that are biased against us with some beans as opposed to no beans.

Is it any wonder that approaches such as the Prospect Theory based approach presented in this chapter are seemingly innate in primates?

CONCLUSION

The paradigm for examining money management that is provided by the Leverage Space Model has afforded us an end that is much more than mere maximization of geometric returns.

It should be pointed out that, even though we seem to approach our allocations and leverage—referring to both manifestations of *"leverage" pointed out earlier in the text*; the immediate snapshot of ratio of quantity to cash, as well as how we progress that ratio through time as equity changes, intimating that leverage, in this second sense, is germane even to a cash account(!)—from an entirely different standpoint than the multiplicative one innate in geometric mean maximization strategies (and thus innate in the Leverage Space Model), we are still somewhere on the terrain of leverage space, only moving along that terrain as our equity changes; the veracity and relevance of that model is unchanged. Rather, the techniques described herein help us to find a path through that terrain, a path that maximizes the probability of profit within a given drawdown constraint, or maximizes profit within both a given drawdown constraint as well as the constraint of a minimum probability of profit. (In fact, without the paradigm provided by the Leverage Space Model and its risk measure of probability of a given drawdown, such approaches would not have been feasible.)

People, including fund managers and individual investors, are *not* wealth maximizers. They are maximizers of probability of profit at some given horizon in time, or maximizers of profit within a given minimum probability of profit, as demonstrated empirically in Prospect Theory, and also further evidenced by the near-universal, visceral reaction exhibited toward the notion of mathematically optimal wealth maximization afforded by geometric mean maximization.

Yet neither the palette nor evolution itself dictate mathematics. Regardless of preferences and attitudes toward risk, everyone exists somewhere on the terrain of leverage space at all times. As a paradigm, the Leverage Space Model allows us to trace a path; it gives us a context upon which to map such paths, and see the results of our actions, to satisfy the (often seemingly pathological) palate of the individual, as exhibited by Prospect Theory, which seeks not to maximize wealth, not to find the highest point in the leverage space landscape, but to trace a path through that landscape so as to maximize the probability of profit at a given future point in time, or operate within a minimum probability of profit.

Further, the Leverage Space Model, since it utilizes the real-world risk metric of drawdown, now permits a small Martingale (demonstrated herein to model the risk preferences of Prospect Theory) to be implemented. We can determine from this what our allocations and progressions of those allocations should be (that is, our "path," through leverage space) so as to accommodate Prospect Theory's *implied* criterion of "maximum probability of profit at a given horizon in time," or, "a requisite minimum tolerable probability of profit in maximizing profit," by determining the functions of such paths through leverage space and those functions' parameters that dictate our path.

We now have a method that allows fund managers to select a horizon in the future whereby they can maximize their probability of profit or of a minimum return, within a given drawdown constraint, in the context of the Leverage Space Model itself. This is but one of an infinite number of possible migration functions, one way of solving for one criterion.

Further, this migration function is not the only way to solve for the optimal probability of profit within a given drawdown constraint by a given time horizon. There are, no doubt, many others. This is not presented as the end-all and be-all, for this criterion. Further, there are innumerable criteria to solve for, and numerous ways of solving for them, some better than others for a given criterion. Hopefully, this serves both as usable migration functions for investors, as well as examples of how to create and implement other migration functions to satisfy other criteria.

You, the analyst or the investor, have your own individual means of utilizing your analysis. You have your own tools of timing and selection in the marketplace, based on given frameworks, be they fundamental, technical, or any other type, and you approach all of this with your own voice, as it were, your own unique method of implementation. It is my hope, then, that within this framework you will find exactly *that:* the tools with which to think freely, a framework wherein you can visualize how the *effects* of *causes* make *sense*, create productive solutions to satisfy the ends you seek—and find your own voice therein.

Bibliography

Aumann, R. J., and M. Maschler. 1985. Theoretic analysis of a bankruptcy problem from the Talmud. *Journal of Economic Theory* **36**: 195–213.

Bellman, R., and R. Kalaba. 1957. On the role of dynamic programming in statistical communication theory. *IEEE Transactions on Information Theory* **3**: 197–203.

Bernoulli, D. 1738. Specimen theoriae novae de mensura sortis (Exposition of a new theory on the measurement of risk). In *Commentarii academiae scientiarum imperialis Petropolitanae* **5**: 175–192. Translated into English: L. Sommer. 1954. *Econometrica* **22**: 23–36.

Bernstein, P. L. 1996. *Against the gods*. New York: John Wiley & Sons, Inc.

Breiman, L. 1961. Optimal gambling systems for favorable games. In *Proceedings of the fourth berkeley symposium on mathematical statistics and probability*, vol. 1, ed. Jerzy Neyman. Berkeley: University of California Press: 65–78.

Chen, K., V. Lakshminarayanan, and L. Santos. 2006. How basic are behavioral differences? Evidence from capuchin monkey trading behavior. *Journal of Political Economy* **114**: 517–537.

Epstein, Richard A. 1967. *The Theory of Gambling and Statistical Logic*. San Diego: Academic Press.

Gehm, F. 1983. *Commodity market money management*. New York: John Wiley & Sons, Inc.

Goldman, M. B. 1974. A negative report on the "near optimality" of the max-expected-log policy as applied to bounded utilities for long lived programs. *Journal of Financial Economics* **1**: 97–103.

Hirashita, Y. 2008. Least-squares prices of coin-flipping games. *International Journal of Applied Mathematics & Statistics* **13**: 3–8.

Hirashita, Y. 2008. A new market model in the large volatility case. *Far East Journal of Applied Mathematics* **32**: 13–20.

Huygens, 1657. *Libellus de ratiociniis in ludo aleae (The value of all chances in games of fortune)*. (Original Latin transcript translated and published in English.) London: S. Keimer for T. Woodward, near the Inner-Temple-Gate in Fleetstreet. 1714.

Kahneman, D., and A. Tversky. March 1979. Prospect theory: An analysis of decision under risk. *Econometrica* **47**: 263–292.

Kelly, J. L., Jr. July 1956. A new interpretation of information rate. *Bell System Technical Journal*: **35**: 917–926.

Keynes, J. M. 1921. *A Treatise on Probability*. London: Macmillan.

Latane, H. A. 1959. Criteria for choice among risky ventures. *Journal of Political Economy* **67**: 144–155.

Latane, H., and D. Tuttle. 1967. Criteria for portfolio building. *Journal of Finance* **22**: 362–363. September.

MacArthur, R. H., and E. R. Pianka. 1966. On the optimal use of a patchy environment. *American Naturalist* **100**: 603–609.

Matsumoto M., and T. Nishimura. 1998. "Mersenne twister: A 623-dimensionally equidistributed uniform pseudo-random number generator," *ACM Transactions on Modeling and Computer Simulation* **8**: 3–30 January 1998

McDermott, R., J. H. Fowler, and O. Smirnov. April 2008. On the evolutionary origin of prospect theory preferences. *Journal of Politics* **79**: (2), 335–350.

Markowitz, H. M. 1952. Portfolio selection. *Journal of Finance* **7**: 77–91.

_____. 1959. *Portfolio Selection: Efficient Diversification of Investments*. New York: John Wiley & Sons, Inc. Cowles Foundation Monograph #16.

_____. 1976. Investment for the long run: New evidence for an old rule. *Journal of Finance* **31**: 1273–1286.

Merton, R. C., and P. A. Samuelson. 1974. Fallacy of the lognormal approximation to optimal portfolio decision-making over many periods. *Journal of Financial Economics* **1**: 67–94.

Pascual, M. J. *Bankroll Control: The Mathematics of Money Management*. Reno, NV: 1987, unpublished.

Press, W. H., B. P. Flannery, S. A. Teukolsky, and W. T. Vetterling. 1986. *Numerical Recipes: The Art of Scientific Computing*. New York: Cambridge University Press, 1986.

Samuelson, P. A. 1971. The "fallacy" of maximizing the geometric mean in long sequences of investing or gambling. *Proceedings of the National Academy of Sciences of the United States of America* **68**: 2493–2496.

_____. 1979. Why we should not make mean log of wealth big though years to act are long. *Journal of Banking & Finance* **3**: 305–307.

Shannon, C. E. 1948. A mathematical theory of communication. *Bell System Technical Journal* **27**: 379–423, 623–656.

Sharpe, W. F. 1963. A simplified model for portfolio analysis. *Management Science* **9**: 277–293.

_____. 1964. Capital asset prices—A theory of market equilibrium under conditions of risk. *Journal of Finance* **19**: 425–442.

Thorp, Edward O. 1962. *Beat the Dealer: A Winning Strategy for the Game of Twenty-One*. New York: Random House.

———. Walden, W. 1966. A winning bet in Nevada baccarat, part I. *Journal of the American Statistical Association* **61**: 313–328.

———. 1971. Portfolio choice and the Kelly criterion. *Proceedings of the 1971 Business and Economics Section of the American Statistical Association* 1972: 215–224. Reprinted 1975 in Stochastic Optimization Models in Finance. 599–620 Academic Press. Edited by W.T. Ziemba. S.L. Brumelle, and R.G. Vickson.

———. The Kelly Money Management System. *Gambling Times* December 1979: 91–92.

Tversky, A., and D. Kahneman. (1981). The framing of decisions and the psychology of choice. *Science* **211**: 453–458.

Vince, R. 2007. *The Handbook of Portfolio Mathematics.* New York: John Wiley & Sons, Inc.

———. 1995. *The New Money Management.* New York: John Wiley & Sons, Inc.

———. 1992. *The Mathematics of Money Management.* New York: John Wiley & Sons, Inc.

———. 1990. *Portfolio Management Formulas.* New York: John Wiley & Sons, Inc.

Von Neumann, J., and O. Morgenstern. 1944. *Theory of Games and Economic Behavior.* Princeton, NJ: Princeton University Press.

Williams, J. B. 1936. Speculation and the carryover. *Quarterly Journal of Economics* **50**: 436–455.

Index